Kindred Faith

KINDRED FAITH

How God works in the lives of His people

LINDSAY SCHULING COOPER

NASHVILLE

NEW YORK • LONDON • MELBOURNE • VANCOUVER

KINDRED FAITH

How God Works in the Lives of His People

Published in New York, New York, by Morgan James Publishing. Morgan James is a trademark of Morgan James, LLC. www.MorganJamesPublishing.com

Scriptures are taken from the Holy Bible, New International Version, NIV. Copyright 1973, 1978, 1984, by Biblica Inc. Used by permission of Zondervan. All rights reserved worldwide. www.zondervan.com. The "NIV" and "New International Version" are trademarks registered in the United States Patent and Trademark Office by Biblica Inc.™

ISBN 9781631951633 paperback
ISBN 9781631951640 eBook
Library of Congress Control Number: 2020937223

Cover Design by:
Christopher Kirk
www.GFSstudio.com

Interior Design by:
Chris Treccani
www.3dogcreative.net

Morgan James is a proud partner of Habitat for Humanity Peninsula and Greater Williamsburg. Partners in building since 2006.

Get involved today! Visit
MorganJamesPublishing.com/giving-back

To my heavenly Father, who graciously chose me for this assignment, and to the people who volunteered their time to share how God has worked in their lives.

CONTENTS

INTRODUCTION

"**P**ick me!" I said while sitting in a circle during Sunday school. That is, to get the crayons, paper, glue, and scissors for our craft after the Bible story. Growing up, my mom and dad took us kids to church every Sunday morning regardless of what the day before looked like. Wednesday night church came next, and the routine went on throughout my childhood. Did I love this? Not especially, but I loved the crafts, cookies, and kind faces that always greeted me. And I got more of all that if I memorized my Bible verses. Even though I was going to church and hearing the stories, they were not taking root in me; they were only stories—or so I thought.

A moment came when my mother sat me down and told me what it meant to be a Christian. Eager to be a good girl, I asked Jesus to come into my life, and even though I remember this prayer, I spent a lot of years lost.

God has a mysterious way of working on us, and throughout the years of college, getting married, teaching art and photography (all those crafts paid off!), and raising a family of my own, I did attend church, but it took a backseat in my life. Sunday was just another day of going to church then moving on to the next day.

In 2014, two things happened to me. First, I started to reflect on my childhood, my teens, and early adulthood regarding what I knew about the Bible. All those stories came flooding back, and I became curious to know where they all fell in line chronologically. Curiosity? I look back now and know it wasn't curiosity, it was God working on me.

Second, I did something I've never done before: I told myself I wanted to make a New Year's resolution for 2015. What could I stick with for one year? Since I had been thinking about the Bible it became clear to me. I was going to read the Bible from beginning to end.

In January I started reading in Genesis, and I read every day. I was fascinated, hooked. One night in February, I asked God, "Lord, use me to do Your works." I prayed this over and over for several nights. Later, I was in my garage and heard a quiet answer: "I want you to interview people and ask them, 'What can you say about God, and how has He worked in your life or changed your life?' And I want you to photograph them."

Everything was so clear on what I needed to do, and it was so perfect because I have always socialized easily with people and love documentary photography. So of course I said yes. With my camera and voice recorder in hand, I went to jails, poor houses, businesses, homes, Hy-Vee (supermarket), and coffee shops, and I listened to the stories of mothers, murderers, gang members, drug dealers, business owners, traitors, war survivors, cancer survivors, and little children. They all had different stories to share, but one common thread ran through them all. They all trusted in our Lord and Savior because they knew that Proverbs 30:5 is true: "Every word of God is pure; He is a shield to those who take refuge in Him."

When I set out to do this project, I was hoping for fifty people because I had such limited time before another school year began. That was me and my expectations—again, self. But no, God had other plans. He had 120 people in mind. It makes me think of what Dr. David Jeremiah once said: "God will never give you an assignment he will not enable you to complete. That is what a spiritual gift is—a supernatural empowering to accomplish the assignment God gives you."

People often ask me, "How did you find all these people?" Well, first off, God found them for me. It was a lot of word-of-mouth and me just boldly going to places I've never been to. I made a lot of phone calls to people I knew and people I didn't know. I always said these same words: "Hello, my name is Lindsay. God has me working on something special. I'd like to interview you and ask you, What can you say about God, and how has He worked in your life/changed your life? And then I'd like to take your portrait."

That was the summer I changed and realized my relationship with Jesus was top priority. He was coming after me, and I didn't stand a chance. When you see how He works in people's lives after they suffer, and He grabs them by the hand so gently, you know without a doubt He is real and He came and He died and He loves all of us despite our sin.

Today I am devoted, in love, a follower, a believer, a transformed woman who will follow my Lord and Savior through any encounter I come upon. I will stumble and sin, but I will do my best to be obedient and shine brightly for Him. He forgives us of any sin because He simply loves us.

I live by this verse from 1 John 2:3-6:

> We know that we have come to know him if we obey his commands. The man who says, "I know him" but does not do what he commands is a liar, and the truth is not in him. But if anyone obeys his word, God's love is truly made complete in him. This is how we know we are in him; whoever claims to live in him must walk as Jesus did.

If you read the Bible, study His Word, pray, and hang out with fellow Christ-followers so you can strengthen one another, you will be changed. God's power will work in you, and you will be transformed. The stories you are about to read testify to this statement I make. I pray this book makes an impact in your life the way it did mine.

Blessings,

Lindsay Schuling Cooper

CHAPTER 1

Change of Heart

How are you still alive? This is what I thought after interviewing each one of these individuals. It is by God's grace they are alive. They all faced trials and hardships due to putting themselves first and God last. It wasn't until they hit rock bottom that they realized they needed to be rescued. And the only One who could rescue them was Jesus Christ.

> "But as for me, I watch in hope for the Lord, I wait for God my Saviour; my God will hear me. Do not gloat over me, my enemy! Though I have fallen, I will rise. Though I sit in darkness, the Lord will be my light. Because I have sinned against him, I will bear the Lord's wrath, until he pleads my case and upholds my cause. He will bring me out into the light; I will see his righteousness."
>
> **Micah 7:7-9**

Dawn

One day when I was thirteen, my cousins came to Des Moines, and we were all going to go to a concert. They were rolling joints of marijuana and drinking, so I joined in. That was my first experience of using, and I liked it. I could never measure up to my older brother, and that always bothered me, but when I was using it didn't seem to bother me at all.

At fourteen I met a boy who invited me to church with him and his family. At the end of the service, they had an altar call. My heart felt pulled, so I went down there and accepted Jesus Christ, but I didn't continue on that path because my family didn't go to church. This is how

Satan works. It was Jesus and me for a minute, and then Satan grabbed me right back. Soon after this, I started smoking weed and drinking again, and I ran around with older kids who had cars.

By the age of fifteen, I had a boyfriend and thought I knew it all. So I moved out of the house, quit school, and got married when I was sixteen. I got pregnant right away and had twin boys when I was seventeen. I was introduced to prescription diet pills from a lady down the hall where I was living. It was like "mother's little helper"; I could take a pill in the morning, go all day long, sleep for a couple of hours, get up, and do the same thing again. I got divorced by the time I was eighteen and was raising the twin boys by myself. I needed to make some money, so I started selling weed. This led to a vicious cycle for the next twenty-plus years. I went from prescription diet pills to white crosses and then to crystal meth. Not only did I use drugs, but I became a dope dealer to make ends meet.

I'm not really sure when it stopped being fun and became necessary. It became a means of survival. I was stuck in a vicious cycle and didn't know how to get out of it. At one time I was in a very abusive relationship, and as I look back I don't know how I'm still sitting here. There were times when the drugs or my boyfriend could have killed me. I just thought it was the normal way of living. He would tell me I was worthless and that I would never amount to anything. If you get told that enough, you start believing it. We were together for almost twenty years, but we never got married because he told me I was not good enough to marry.

At one point I made it another thirteen years without getting into any trouble. That was about to come to an end. However, God was in full control. The people I had gotten my drugs from had just gotten busted about a month before that, and my plan was to wean myself off. I really doubt that would have worked, but that's what I thought at the time.

I was sitting at home with my little brother and my granddaughter when I heard something hit the back door. I thought, *My ex got out of prison, and nobody told me!* So I jumped up and went to the back door. It was the Des Moines police—and I had a lot of drugs in the house.

I went to jail and was looking at fifty years in prison—twenty-five years for the drugs and twenty-five years for the guns. Again, God knew what to do because, the night before, I had cleaned out my bedroom and thrown everything in the spare room, which had a safe in it. The safe had $11,000 in it. They opened that bedroom door and glanced inside. It was such a mess that it looked as though they had already been through it.

When I was sitting in jail, I started praying and didn't realize I was doing the first three steps of the Narcotics Anonymous program. My life was out of control. I was locked behind bars and had a $140,000 bond. I prayed, *Dear God, please help me. I don't know what to do, but You have my full attention.* I always believed in Him, but I was not doing what He wanted me to do. I prayed, *You need to show me something different. Please show me something different because I can't do this anymore. I don't want my granddaughter to visit me behind bars.* The next day, they reduced my bond, and I got out with some of the money I had stashed. I heard a voice asking me, "What are you going to do? Are you going to buy more drugs? Are you going to get yourself out of this trouble that you got yourself into?" I decided the second thought was a much better choice. I'm sure it was God's voice that I heard.

I put myself into an outpatient treatment program. I can see God in everything. The reason I had the money was because God knew what I would do with it. If I had some drugs left, I might have gone back to that life, but the cops took them all away. Again, thank You, Lord!

God brought me to Narcotics Anonymous, and NA brought me closer to God. The program uses spiritual steps that mention a higher power because they don't want to tell you what God to believe in. I knew it was Jesus the whole way.

I went to the meetings and felt right at home because I was with people who were like me. It's what I had been looking for all those years. Before this, I could wear whatever mask I wanted to wear for whatever time I needed to wear it to get whatever I needed to get.

After I had been clean for over ninety days, my lawyer called and said, "I think I can get you a plea bargain. Meet me down at the courthouse." It was a Friday morning in May—three months after I got busted. I went, and he came out and told me, "I think somebody made the judge mad. He's going to give you a plea bargain of eight years." A friend who was with me said, "If she takes the plea bargain, can she get her affairs in order before she goes to prison?" My lawyer said, "Let me go find out." By this time, I was on the courtroom floor crying, praying, and begging God not to let this happen. I had over ninety days clean, which was a miracle because I could not get even three days clean when I was using. I prayed, "Lord, You have to help me. I don't know what to do. I don't want to go to prison for fifty years, but eight years feels like a life sentence too."

Then I heard a voice say, "You've come this far. You are not going to lay down and take this. Get up and fight." So I stood up, literally brushed myself off, and said, "Well, if you are going to throw me in prison, you will have to do it next week because I have an NA meeting to chair tonight, and I'm going to be there." I went to the meeting and told them, "If I'm not here next Friday, it's because I'm in prison. It's not because I don't want to be here." A bunch of people wrote letters for me to the judge, and I know it was all God's plan. It still amazes me to think that God loves me so much when I thought I was so worthless. I'm still nothing without Him. I went to court and was sitting there writing down the twelve steps of NA. I prayed, "God, I'm scared. I don't know what to do." The light kind of flickered. I felt like it was Him letting me know, "I'm here. You are not alone, My dear child." I went to trial, and they found me guilty of just possession. They still wanted to give me eight years, but I ended up getting three years' probation and a $2,000 fine. Thank You, Jesus!

Now I'm really involved in NA, and I'm allowed to have meetings at the Polk County Jail. It's all because of the grace of God that He allows me to do that. The DOC wanted me to live there. Jesus wants me to take meetings there to let people know they don't have to keep doing this.

The day before my trial was the day I got saved. On Saturday night, while I was at an NA meeting, two girls in the room told me there was going to be an evangelist at Grace Church. They were going on Sunday and wanted me to go. I got to the church that morning and looked around. The two girls were not there. I decided I was already there, so I went in. A guy named Rick Amato was speaking about how he'd been a heroin and cocaine addict and had now been clean for twenty-five years. At one point in his life, he was lying in a hospital bed with tubes coming out of his body from an overdose and was pretty much dead. He remembers telling God, "If You pull me through this, I will do nothing but live for You."

The evangelist then said, "There's somebody out in the audience. I don't know who, but there is a mountain in front of you, and you don't know how to get over it. There's no way over it, and there is no way around it." I thought, *Yes, that's the truth*. The more he talked, the more I felt like he was talking to me. He then asked for everyone to close their eyes. He said, "If anyone would like to accept Christ, now is the time to do it because He can get you over that mountain. He can get you through that mountain, and He can get you around that mountain. Whatever He has got to do, He can do it. He can knock it out of your way." The next thing I knew, I was standing up, and he said, "Open your eyes." He called us forward, and I accepted Christ that day. This was the day before the trial—May 21, 2000.

I knew Jeff way back in the day when we were all using. I didn't know him really well, but I knew him. Our lives reconnected in 2010. From that moment we became best friends and have been together as a couple since February 2011.

On November 30, 2015, my son, Bryon, and his fiancé, Heather, were murdered while they were sleeping. My grandson, Brylee, was six weeks old and lying in his mom's arms when she was shot. He and my granddaughter, Peyton, were in the house for anywhere from four to eight hours before they were found.

My life was turned upside down and inside out. I could see God's preparation in all of this. I don't blame God at all. He gave us all free will, and some use it for evil. They arrested the man three days later. The next morning, while doing my morning meditations, I forgave that man. If I didn't, I would become bitter, not better. That is not for me to carry. God is in charge, not me. It was one of the hardest things I've ever had to do in my life.

Life is harder now without my son; however, God is always in control. Both Bryon and Heather accepted Christ, so I know they are in a much better place. I realize this is something I will never get over, but with God's love, grace, and mercy I can cope because of the hope I have in Jesus Christ. I will see him again someday.

Every day at work I still try and spread the light of Jesus and leave the results to God. I have no idea what God has in store for me; however, I talk with Him every day, praise Him, and pray because I know my life is in His hands, every second of every day.

I had no idea that God would take a sinner like me, pluck me from Satan's hands, and place me on holy ground. For years I wanted to die, and I am so very grateful that He didn't let me die in active addiction. I would have missed out on so many blessings, trials, and convictions that make me the person I am today.

Don't think that God can't change you because He can. We just have to let Him. I'm living proof that God can take all we've done wrong, no matter how terrible we think it is, and use it for His good. I am living proof and a walking miracle, only because of Jesus!

Jeff

I grew up in a farmhouse with very hardworking parents who both did a good job of raising all nine of us kids. Where I grew up was pretty drug-infested, and that's where I was introduced to drugs—at the age of thirteen. This was in 1974.

I never really went to church and never thought about God, but one of my older brothers, Danny, was a Christian and in the military by the time I was a teenager. When I was seventeen, we went out to see him in Virginia for two weeks, and he talked to me about God. That was my first introduction to God. He talked to me a lot about it. I wanted to stop smoking pot and doing all that stuff. Yet I came home and went right back to where I was. Still, he planted that seed, and I remember it.

After I graduated from high school, my high school sweetheart got pregnant, so we married and had a boy named Donnie. Soon after our marriage, we went our separate ways. She was my first love, and it just tore me up. That's when my drug addiction really started. I didn't like to sleep at night because I would lie in bed and think about things. I don't like talking about it because it was such a treacherous time in my life.

So, after starting drugs at thirteen, I continued on that same path for thirty-five years. Drugs were a part of my everyday life. Then I got into making drugs—meth. About seven years ago, I was living in the basement of a drug house and making meth when a fire started. I tried to put it out, but I couldn't. I've always been a tough guy and able to do anything. I remember thinking, *Oh my gosh, I'm going to die. I'm done.* I gave up; I just couldn't do it. I was burning, and I went to the ground. I don't remember anything except, all of a sudden, I stood up and the fire was out. I looked down the hallway and saw two or three white shadows floating out the door. To this day, I can't tell you what I saw. Angels? At that moment, I knew there was a God.

They took me to the hospital, and I lied to them. I told them I was cooking dinner and it exploded. When I got home, I called my brother Danny and told him about my experience. He started to talk to me about God and Jesus again. It was overwhelming.

All during this time, I was still getting high. That's what addiction does. But God is strong; He intervened even when I was getting high. I was going to court for a manufacturing (drug) charge and thought for sure I was headed to prison. When I went to court to be sentenced, however, the judge who wanted to sentence me was on vacation, so they had another judge. She told me that if I went into in-jail treatment at the Polk County Jail and succeeded in that, I could get probation and might not have to go to prison. I was in awe. I couldn't believe it. So they arrested me on the spot. I remember getting handcuffed in the courtroom knowing my life was going to change.

The first thing I did when I got to jail was put in a request for a pastor I had met awhile back (he knew my brother). He came to see me and brought me a Bible. When I was in that place, they would shut the lights off at night. You're supposed to be in your cell and in your bed at a certain time. Every night I would take my Bible and go to the end of the cell where the hallway was and read it. I wasn't supposed to be out there, but the guard let me. I didn't understand all of it, but I kept reading the Bible because I knew there was a God and I needed to get closer to Him.

I was always the black sheep of my family. When I was in jail, I wrote all my brothers, my sister, and my ex-wife and told them where I was, what I was doing, and how my life was about to change because God was going to change it for me. Sure enough, He did. The power of God is unbelievable. He took somebody like me, even with all I've done over all those years, and gave me the gifts I presently have. It is just unbelievable.

I succeeded in the program and had to go back to court to be sentenced. I was pretty sure I was going to prison, but I knew that whatever God's plan was for me, that's where I was going. The judge asked me if I wanted to address the court. I said, "Yes, I sure do. I want to thank you for allowing me to go to the in-jail treatment program and for the opportunity to start life over, to see my son, and most of all to be with my Father God and to serve Him." The judge said, "Are you done, Mr. Davis?" I said, "Yes, sir." He said, "Well, let me tell you something. If I ever see you here again, I will send you to prison, but I am going to honor what the other judge said."

I got out of treatment and went right back to the drug house where I was living before. But God gave me the strength not to do drugs and to start my life over again. To this day, I still have problems praying because of what I did for all those years. I don't read the Bible like I should, but I attend church every Sunday and talk to people about God. When I think of where I am today and where I was ten years ago, I know that I could not have done that on my own. There is only one way.

God intervened in my life. My brother told me that being a Christian is the hardest thing you will ever do, but I strive for it every day. When I started going to Grace Church, I didn't know that the pastor who prayed with me would be there. He asked me if I wanted to be in his class, and I said sure. He said the best thing ever to me, and I will never forget it. He said, "Let's grow old and love Jesus." It is not a coincidence that these people are in my life. It's not that I planned it, but Somebody did.

I want to end with a story. My mom was the strongest woman I've ever known. You always have this impression that your mom is going to make it through anything because moms are strong, taking care of everything and everyone. When she got sick with cancer, one day I went to see her at the hospital. My sister came out of the room with the nurse, crying. I said, "What's going on?" Marty couldn't really talk to me, so I asked the nurse what was going on. The nurse said, "Your mom is probably not going to make it through the night." I said, "What are you talking about?" She said, "I suggest you call the family."

So I called all my brothers and told them the news. Danny said he'd fly into Omaha. The other brothers, who all live out-of-state, could not make it, even though the one with the least amount of money could make it. I never said anything to Mom after I talked to my brothers. She looked at me and said, "Jeffrey, I'm not going to make it this time." I said, "That's okay, Mom. We are alright." She said, "When are you going to get Danny?" I said, "How did you know I'm going to get him?" She said, "Well, moms know these things, but I will see you when you get back."

When we got back from Omaha, Danny and I walked into her room. She was sitting up like she was going to live for another ten years. About an hour later, I remember her sitting in that bed saying, "Oh God, oh God," and looking in the corner like she was seeing something. It scared me. We all left, and Danny was the only one in there. It was around four o'clock in the morning when she passed away. Danny told me that she believed, so we will see her again someday. I always thought it was so weird that she waited for Danny. That whole God thing in the corner has stuck with me too, and I always wondered, what did she see? I wasn't a Christian at that time, so I didn't understand at all. Now I do.

Jerry

I was raised in church all of my childhood and young adult years. During my junior year of high school, I got engaged to a young woman, but I didn't want to follow through with the marriage so I moved to California. I don't know if I really considered myself a Christian. I just thought of myself as a religious person because of my church background.

I moved 1800 miles away from my family to where my older brother lived in California. I was into athletics in school, so I wasn't involved with any of the things that most young people were doing, like drugs, alcohol, and smoking. After living with him for a couple of weeks, I moved into an apartment so I could go to college. The apartment complex manager befriended me and invited me to her church's college-age youth group. I decided to take her up on that because, as I look back, God was working in my life to cause me to want Him.

The Vietnam War was going on at that time, and I didn't want to go to Vietnam. They used a lottery to choose those who were going. I began to pray after getting connected with this youth group and started watching TV on Sundays with various speakers. I was fascinated by the way they seemed to worship and know God. I was really crying out to God about Vietnam and not wanting to go. I made an oath, at that time, about my beard. I told God I would shave it if my lottery number was high. I made a promise to Him, and He answered my prayer. My number was very high. They didn't draft up to that number, so I didn't go to Vietnam. I shaved my beard to honor the commitment and oath I had made to God. When God did that I felt, for once in my life, He answered a specific prayer and was becoming more personal to me. Looking back, I remember that whole answer to prayer as building trust. I could trust God.

The church I attended was Southern Baptist, and it was the first time in my life I had heard the gospel: Jesus died for me, shed His blood, and rose from the dead. I remember having an urge to go forward to receive Christ, but a voice came into my head and said, *Christians don't have fun. Don't go do that.* It was enough to stop me, and I said no to God.

I moved back to Iowa, and God continued to work in my life. For the next year, I went through a series of things that were really hard. At the same time, God placed people in my life. One man, named Lowell, became an instant friend. You can imagine my surprise when I found out he led the choir at his church.

I said, "What? You're too cool to lead the choir." I was blown away that this really sharp guy was leading a choir in his church! He invited me out to play golf and to his house where he shared the four spiritual laws with me: 1) God loves you, 2) Man is sinful and separated from God, 3) Jesus Christ is God's only provision for man's sin, and 4) We must individually receive Jesus as Savior and Lord. Once again, I was confronted with accepting Christ, and I said no.

Then he invited me to come to church with him, so I went to the church for several weeks. One day he told me I didn't have a chance because the whole church was praying for me. On Friday nights, all the college and high school students got together. There were about two hundred in that church, and it was just so alive you couldn't get away from God when He was working in your life. One Friday night, I looked up into the sky after a football game and took notice of what Romans 1 says: "God has created the universe to declare that He is real, and that He is at work in people's lives." As I looked up, the planets and stars were in majestic order, and I heard His voice say, *If I can arrange the entire universe, I think I can handle your puny life.*

At that moment, I prayed the sinner's prayer. I asked Jesus into my heart, to forgive me of my sins and to fill me with the Holy Spirit. That was in September 1972, and from that point on, God's been at work in my life. The youth group we were involved in was so alive! They were out sharing their faith. They read and consumed more and more of God's Word. It was a holy time to be a part of it all. Two weeks later, I was immersed (baptized in obedience to the Word of God). I will never forget what happened when I got baptized. I remembered reading that God's words came to Jesus at His baptism: "This is My Son, whom I love; with him I am well pleased." I heard His voice say, *Jerry, you are My son, and I am well pleased.* That was the first step to obedience.

Since then it's always been a passion of mine to be in ministry. I tried going off to Bible college, but my character was not yet near what it needed to be in order to be in ministry. I was an immature mess emotionally, in my life and character. It was thirty years after high school before I earned my college degree. At that point, I was working in a church called Grace Church. It was a privilege to finish my degree and prepare for ministry. Patty and my kids felt that I was ready to be a pastor and leader in the church, so I took that step of faith. The pastors and elders at Grace Church ordained me, and I was called to the Newton Prison facility to work in Chuck Colson's Prison Fellowship Ministry. I faithfully served there for nearly four years. After it closed down, I was called to be the chaplain at the Polk County Jail and have been there for over ten years.

I'm so excited to work with an assistant chaplain and thirty-two committed volunteers. Through the power of the Holy Spirit, we have all sowed the seed of God's Word and watched literally hundreds of people come to saving faith in Jesus Christ. I am very honored to see how God has worked over the years to develop me for the assignments He has planned for me. He does not waste any of our experiences, any of our faults, or any of our many frailties. He molds and shapes us into the men and women that His Holy Spirit can greatly use, and He gives us a burden to be used. To God be the glory!

Tony

While growing up, I raced bicycles, mostly on Sundays. So my church life, my Christian life, was nonexistent. I met a lot of kids while racing, which led to bad habits. I never got into heavy drugs, but I smoked a lot of pot. That carried all the way to high school, and that's how I made money.

As I entered high school, I started drinking and did a fair amount of drugs too. Recently, I went on Facebook to look for old friends and found no one. Then I went to IAMUGSHOTS.COM and found a lot of people I graduated with. Many of them kept moving in the same direction with drugs and alcohol and never stopped.

Like so many people I got married and went through a painful divorce. Shortly after my wife moved out, I remember being in bed, feeling a hand on my thigh, and hearing the words *It's going to be alright.* I thought I was dreaming it or going crazy. To this day, I know that was God. He didn't give up on me. There are a lot of reasons why He could have said, "You are done." I'm one that needs a slap on the head to get something through to me. As I look back on it, I see He footprints.

After all of that, I started to get my head on straight and wanted to find somebody else. So I did the bar thing; I had no other method. My cousin had also gone through a divorce. She told me to come to a Bible study group in Norwalk for single people. Since I hadn't learned much about the Bible while growing up, I was biblically illiterate. I tried it for a while, and it kept me in God's Word. However, at the time I felt like my world was falling in on me. After my divorce, I thought I was going to lose my house and possibly be homeless. At one point I needed $1,500. My mom sent out a prayer chain to their church. Somebody stepped forward and handed them a check. When it was given to me, it was given anonymously. I tried to find out who sent it, but I had no luck.

When I look back on it, everything fit into place. The money allowed me to stay in that house long enough to meet Shell. Otherwise, our paths never would have crossed because I would have moved. We lived different kinds of lives, and there's no way we would have met. I might have thought she was a good catch, but she would have looked at me and said, "No way."

I thought the normal thing to do after you start dating someone seriously is to move in together to see if it works. We sat down one night, and I proposed the idea. I said, "Listen, we are serious about each other. Let's move in together and see how we function together as a couple." Her response was, "No way, not doing it." For a while, I questioned that. If we were going to get married, it would have been like a test, a trial run. But, no, she wouldn't do it. Shell was who God saw for me way back. Her parents and all the family got me on the right track. Everything needed to happen the way it happened for me to be where I am today.

If someone had looked at me in high school and said, "In twenty-two years, you'll be a deacon at a church," I would have laughed. It's very interesting to look back on how things happened. At the time, it doesn't make sense, but as time goes on it does. I see why things needed to happen the way they happened. Now I'm very much involved in church. With the way I was going, I probably would have survived, but I would have just existed. God never gave up on me. He knows my future. Today I have a relationship with Him, and I turn to Him for everything.

Irene

My two sisters and I grew up in orphanages because my father killed himself when I was five and my mom couldn't take care of us—she turned to drinking because she blamed herself.

We lived in a private orphanage called Moose Heart in Illinois, sponsored by the Moose Lodge. Moose Heart was like its own little city—a city full of orphans. It's gated, and you live in different houses based on your age. I didn't live with my sisters, just girls my age. I was there from the ages of five to eight until my mom met the man who I now consider my dad.

We were taken out of there and brought home, but my mom and dad both drank and did drugs, so we were right back in that same toxic environment. They were the first people to give me drugs. I smoked weed with my parents when I was in second and third grades. I thought that was the norm. I thought all kids went to school stoned. Things didn't go well at home because of their addictions and going to bars. We ended up going back to the orphanage for another year and a half. During that time, my mom and dad stopped using and drinking, got married, and joined the Mormon Church. I was baptized Mormon when I was eight years old while living in the orphanage. I knew there was a God, but I never knew what baptism was. I just knew that I was forgiven of my sins. The only religion I knew was the Mormon religion, and we learned all these religious practices based on the Mormon religion.

My sisters and I all fell away from the church in our early teens. They started partying, so I did too. I left home when I was fifteen over an incident with my father, who looked at me through a hole in the shower. It was a horrible incident, but I have forgiven him. He was the only person I had as a dad, so I loved him. He was my best friend, and we played ball together. That is one of my fondest memories. I had a real connection/bond with him, and I never understood why that happened.

I moved in with my boyfriend, who eventually became my husband. All I ever did was drink and do drugs because I suffered from a lot of abandonment issues. It was my way of not feeling. I could shut my feelings off very easily when I got high and drunk. That's what I've done all my life. I got pregnant when I was sixteen, married at seventeen, and divorced a year later. I left my husband because I didn't really know what love was. I had a taste for the wild life so the state took my child from me, and I clung to the next drug dealer.

Men have always been a weakness in my life because I never really had much of a father figure. I was always looking for love, and I looked in all the wrong places. As soon as I left my first husband, I hooked up with a guy who would become my next husband. It was all based on drugs and alcohol, so it was very violent. I was constantly abused and lost my identity. Then I started suffering because of the guilt of not having my son. I got pregnant and had a couple of abortions. The man I was with said I had to do it. I had just lost my son to the state and thought, *How can I have another kid when I can't even take care of the one I have?* Because of my religion, I knew I would go to hell for that, but I chose to do it anyway. At that point in my life, I settled for the fact that I'd done things and that God did not love me. I developed guilt and shame and everything that goes along with it.

After I left my second husband, I went directly to the person who would end up becoming the father of my next two children. I stayed with him for thirteen years. We never got married because I thought, *I'm not going to do this again.* We lived together, and he was a drug dealer. This man ended up going to prison when my girls were five and six. Before he left, he had an affair with my best friend. I never imagined in my wildest dreams he'd do that to me. When he went to prison, he left me with two kids, a meth lab, and a broken heart. I think that kind of destroyed me as far as men. Everything turned for me, and I got very cold. I did the only thing I thought was possible to survive, the only thing I knew: I sold meth. I made drugs and sold them. I had live-in nannies. I was never with my kids. I took care of them well, but not the way they needed to be taken care of. I'm suffering now from a lot of that stuff. They needed me. They had everything but me.

In 2008, I got rescued, as I now call it. Arrested for selling meth, I was in big trouble and knew I was going to prison. I was miserable. I hated life. I was doing things I wasn't okay with, and I had crossed every boundary I ever had. You start out with boundaries and things you are not okay with, but in your progression you cross every single boundary you had. I hated myself. I was completely broken.

In the Polk County Jail I met a pastor. He was the first pastor to ever tell me I didn't have to go to hell. He told me that if I asked Christ into my life, asked for forgiveness from my sins, and turned from them I could be forgiven and saved. I can't even explain the relief those words provided me. So I did it; I asked Christ into my life and got saved. I was still going to prison, but I was released from all of that. I started praying. I met other chaplains and pastors. They were huge inspirations to me. I spent ten months in Polk County Jail before I went to prison. While there, I did Bible studies, memorized Scripture, learned from the pastors, and got close to the Lord. It's amazing that, through all this stuff, I never lost my children. God always provided a way. Even when I went to prison, DHS was not involved. People came along and took care of my kids. I never had to get child support. They were safe.

It's easy to be close to the Lord when you don't have the distractions of the world. I spent my whole time while locked up having complete peace. He walked me through the whole time. I can't even explain how He walked me through that. He had my back, and He took care of everything for me. It's amazing when I think about the grace and mercy He showed me.

When I got out of prison, I lived in a halfway house for six months, and one of the things I've realized now is that I'm very passionate about helping women when they are coming out. You've got to have that support. When you are used to living a lie and then come out, you don't know what to do.

Satan is conniving and very clever. He knows exactly how to get you. I came out into the world not really knowing what to do or having a plan. Satan hit me as hard as he could. The world smacked me in the face, and I struggled. I wanted to do the right things, but I didn't know how. I had changed, but no one else around me had. I came out and was so excited, but nobody else was. Over and over I would get rejected, and nobody was on board. No one wanted to do what I wanted to do. It became very heartbreaking. Eventually, a man came into my life, and I fell. The amazing thing about God is that He disciplines His children. Once you are a child of God, you are His kid. I would tell Him all the time, "Don't give up on me." But I was doing the same things I was used to doing.

I went back to using. God would let me go a little bit, and then He'd sit me right back in Polk County Jail to start all over again. God didn't say He wanted part of me. He said He wanted all of me. I thought I could live

a certain way and abide by some of the rules, but I didn't want to give it all up. I would hold onto sexual immorality because I would get with these boyfriends. I wanted to be happy, be in love, and be all these things, but I wasn't doing it the right way. Satan knew my weaknesses, and he would throw me into the worst possible situations. He was slick at it. He would send a boyfriend who would say, "Sure, we can go to church, whatever you want." But it would never end up that way. Satan is sneaky and would use those subtle little twists.

I went back to Polk County Jail. I went back to prison and sat in the hole. I spent a lot of time with God. Each time, I came out a little bit stronger, and I gave up a little bit more. Every time I went to Polk County, the chaplain would always be there to smile at me and tell me he was glad to see me, but not in jail. He'd fill me with the Word. Then I'd go back to prison for a month and sit in the hole with just myself and God. I'd read and repent. I'd say, "Okay, God, let's try this again."

At some point I got arrested again and then rescued again and went back to Polk County Jail. I was actually relieved. I walked into a Bible study and met Denise, who led the study. She carried the Spirit so strong. I looked at the girl next to me and said, "She's going to be my best friend, and she doesn't even know it. I'm attaching myself to her hip." I decided that something was going to change. I needed to surrender. I thought, *Okay, God, here I am. Do with me whatever You want. I will give it all up, and I won't be sexually immoral. I won't drink, use…any of it.* He immediately filled me, and I spent six weeks in Polk County Jail going to Bible studies and attaching myself to this woman. I started teaching Bible studies on my own and sharing the story of salvation. I went back to prison and back into the hole where I sat and waited for a judge. I was all alone, which was what I needed. I spent so much time with God and getting my mind right. When I had my Bible study, I would share about my life.

God works in crazy ways. I always prayed that He would let me come home as soon as possible. But I didn't want my will, I wanted His will. They took me in front of the board, and they said that after I did a drug treatment program, I could go up for parole, which would be in four or five months. Two days later, I got a letter in the mail that said, "Your parole application was entered in error. It's going to be expunged from your record, and you have to have a hearing." I thought, *Does that mean they goofed? Now they can't put me behind the gates because they goofed!*

Long story short, I had a court hearing on August 5 and told the lawyer, "Will you please call my parole officer and tell her that I realize what I did was wrong. I'm really sorry. I have a home to go to and a job to go to. Would you consider letting me out?" I spent the next six weeks waiting. During this time my sister was also there, and it gave me the opportunity to share with her about Christ. I told her we needed to change our lives. I went to the hearing on August 5, and my parole officer said, "It's okay. You can go home." It was totally a God thing. He softened her heart and gave me grace again. I thought, *Okay, now let's see what You are going to do. I already know, but let's just see.* I was home within five days, and I could have been in prison for five more months. God allowed me to come home.

I moved in with my sister-in-law and started going to church. I got involved in Denise's Tuesday night Bible study, and my life has changed 180 degrees. I gave it all up, and my husband and I decided we were going to make it work—even though he was still incarcerated. He knows more about the Bible than I do. We study the Word together and do devotionals together. We talk three times a day and visit four times a week.

I have such a passion for addicts. Last week I got a call from a woman named Mary at CrossRoads Ministry. They minister to the halfway houses. She was resigning from the board of directors and wanted to know if I'd be willing to take her place. She said, "I talked to the chaplain about you, and we would like to meet with you." So I met with them and shared my story. I was asked to be on the board for CrossRoads to help minister to women at the halfway houses. I prayed about it, and I'm going to do it. God put me in this position at this time because I am bold in speaking about my faith. I want to tell everyone about Jesus, but obviously I wasn't always like this. He's done so much for me, so why wouldn't I share that? There are many hurting people in prison who are coming out. I pick up women who have gotten out and take them to church. I tell them, "Come and try it out. You don't have to come back." I bring them, but it's God who has to do the work.

A friend of mine who went back to prison has a Suburban. I said, "Dave, I need a bigger car. I can't get all these people to church." He said, "You know, Irene, you have changed so much. Go to my house. I have a Suburban there. Drive it around for a while and see if you like it. If you do, give me $25 a week, and you can have it." After a while, I had paid him like $900. On my birthday, he called me and said, "I'm so proud of you. You are doing great things. You can have the car." These are the things God does when you are trying to do the right thing.

God sees everything I do, and I don't want to disappoint Him. If I keep my eyes on Him, and I'm doing what He wants me to do, everything else will work out. I have good relationships with my kids, even though I've let them all down. They grew up in the worst lifestyle, but they aren't into drugs. They hate meth. They are starting to trust me a little more. They've been waiting to see if it's real or not. My daughter and granddaughter come to church with me. I'm in four Bible studies a week, and they are all praying for me and my family. I do the Bible studies, but I also work alongside my mentor because I want to learn from her. We listen to Christian music while we paint and remodel houses.

These are the things that keep me balanced. Most people might need one dose of something. Well, I need ten! It keeps me grounded. Satan throws people from my past at me in order to get me distracted, but I choose to surround myself with Christians because they are a positive influence. I want to honor God. How could you not? Every day I stand in awe.

Jarvis and Connie

Jarvis's Story:

I come from a family of eighteen kids: ten boys, eight girls. I was third from the youngest. My father was a truck driver and would go on long international road trips, so my mom raised us all. My father was a very spiritual man. We could not leave the house and go to school, work, or play until we all had gathered around the table for Bible study.

My mother was a very caring mother even though she was a functioning alcoholic. She would get up, get us ready for school or church, and feed us. She made sure we had food, and she was a very strict mother. If you see a mother duck with her chicks behind, that's how she was. I was probably twelve when I really noticed her addiction. At the time, I didn't think much of it because we were all fine. But as the years passed, I started to notice more of it, and then the health issues started. She developed liver disease, but before she passed away she stopped drinking. I lost my mom when I was seventeen because of alcoholism.

As an adolescent, I wanted to venture out and do different things. I wanted to do *me*, but doing me just did not work. By the grace of God, I am sitting here today because those were some very dangerous times that I had no business making it out of. I know God was protecting me because He had something for me to do; it is what I am doing today. I used to tell people I wish I had changed a long time ago, but then I thought, *No, that was not God's plan.* We have to go through some mess sometimes to see that God will bless us. He allows us to go through that mess, but some of us don't make it.

Substance abuse runs rampant through my family. I started with marijuana at the age of fourteen because my brothers did it. Whenever they went out, I would sneak into their room and find their stuff because I knew they were doing it. When I was nineteen, I started drinking, but I never really liked it. I just did it because my peers and friends were doing it. When I was about twenty-five, I started crack cocaine. I always told myself I would never do that, but I saw everyone else doing it. I held back for a long time. I vowed never to touch it, but I did.

I got addicted to crack for about twenty years. There were times when the drugs were so consuming I would lose jobs. I would find another job and stay with it for a while, but the drugs were more important than my job. They were more important than anything. When I was out there addicted to drugs and alcohol, I came to kill, steal, and destroy. I hated people. When I looked at them, I saw them as prey. I never killed anyone, but I shot people. I have been shot myself. When people saw me, they locked their doors and shut their curtains. Nobody wanted me around. I became homeless at several points in my life because nobody accepted me or wanted me around. It got so bad that sometimes I would see an abandoned house and break in just to lie down and go to sleep at night. I would check car doors so I could get out of the cold.

I was incarcerated in 2008 due to drug addiction and drug dealing, and while at the Polk County Jail I got into a Bible study program. At one point, they offered me two programs: one for thirty days and another for ninety days. I was a wreck when I came here and knew I needed something long-term. They offered me Bridges and told me it was a spiritual faith-based program. I prayed about it and felt like God was saying, *Go there. I have something there for you.* I thought about it for two weeks and prayed on it then decided to join the program because I knew I needed it. I wanted to stay in tune and in touch with God because I knew I needed to gather some strength before I was released. There was still a lot of darkness in me.

I started participating in the Bridges program, a bit reluctant at first because I still had that street mentality. I have a sister who is very spiritual. About two or three years before I got incarcerated she said, "Jarvis, one day, God has it on my heart that you are going to be a preacher." I laughed at her because I was so evil and dark inside. I thought, *Are you kidding me? I want nothing to do with God.* At the time she said that, I had a pocket full of money, a big sack of dope, and a beer in my left hand. I remember this very vividly, and I think God has given me that image so I can weigh the difference and always see that I never want to go back into that darkness. I thought she was being ridiculous because why would I stand in front of a group of people and speak on something I knew nothing about and something I didn't want to know anything about. But today I am a minister.

I have a position as the second Sunday minister at Sunshine Open Bible; I am also an usher there and just do whatever else the church calls me to do. I went to Iowa School of Ministry through the Iowa Ministry Network for a while and then did some online stuff. After studying for about five years, I decided to get my ordination. I mentored a lot of guys, but I still didn't know my purpose. I really felt the calling when I started standing up to people and talking about Christ and giving my testimony.

When I saw that my testimony helped other people testify, I thought, *Oh, wow, maybe God wants me to keep telling people so they can see there is a change if you give your life over to Christ. There is a better way.*

It says in Scripture, "I am the way, the truth, and the life. No one comes to the Father except through me." I used to live by that, and I knew I needed to get in tune with Jesus Christ first before I could even see or know anything about the glorious Father. I had some work to do. That was an awesome moment when I saw that my testimony really helped people come out of their shells.

Connie – People used to say to me, "You are dating who? Do you know what he does?" His sister-in-law was my best friend, and we lived in the same apartment complex. She called me one night and said, "My brother-in-law is in treatment now, and I think you two would be a good match." They were both going to NA meetings, and he was in the Bridges program. She showed him a picture of me, and he said, "Yeah, I'll talk to her." She sent me a picture, we started talking, and we've been together since 2009.

At first I didn't really know him. I couldn't see him because he was in the Bridges program, so we would spend hours on the phone, and we wrote letters. I took care of his kids. Their mom was trapped in that world of darkness and destruction. He called me one night from Bridges crying because they could not find their mom and had nothing to eat. He said, "I need you to go get my kids." I went and picked them up that night, bought them clothes and shoes, and had them the whole summer.

Jarvis – I knew she was a keeper when I saw that. We got custody of them, and we've had them for five years. Again, she had only met me but didn't really know much about me. We got married on 11/11/11 at 11:11. This is the healthiest relationship I've ever been in, and I'm fifty-two years old.

Connie's Story:

I don't even remember what year I became addicted to drugs—probably around 1996. I was a drug dealer, one of the best in Ohio, and a single mother. All the people I was dealing for were getting busted on the highway while bringing me the drugs. The DEA was busting everybody, and I knew I was probably next. I got really scared because I was concerned about what would happen to my kids. If I got caught, I knew they would either go back to their father, who they never saw, or go live with my parents—or they would go into the system.

One night I woke up suddenly and was scared to death. I started packing my house, getting rid of all the drugs and all the money—which was a lot. I had money hidden in laundry detergent boxes. I had mattresses cut up and money hidden in there. Money was hidden behind pictures. I would get so high that I'd hide money and not even know I'd hid it. I held a job because I knew I had to account for the money because I would just go buy cars whenever I wanted.

Two days later, my neighbors, an elderly couple, got raided. The police had gone to the wrong house. I knew my time was coming. I just kept getting worse and worse, and I was so addicted that I could not even cook for my kids. I would take the cocaine and cook it to make crack cocaine. I was snorting it and smoking it. When I finally moved to Des Moines, I moved in the middle of the night and didn't tell a soul I was leaving. I packed my kids up in the car with a duffel bag for me and a duffel bag for them and left. I left everything. That's when I stopped doing drugs. I quit cold turkey, even cigarettes. In February 2008, I stopped drinking alcohol. I knew that if I did not change my life, I was going to lose everything I had.

I became a Christian because of Jarvis. We had been talking for about fifteen minutes when he said, "Now we are going to get into the questions." I figured it was going to be sexual questions because that's normally what guys ask. I was like, *Oh, great. Here we go.* Then he said, "Do you believe in God?"

I said, "Yes, I went to church with my grandma when I was younger."

He said, "Would you go to church with me?"

"I don't know, Jarvis."

"Don't worry; you won't burst into flames when you step into the church. Well, you think about it and let me know. Goodnight."

I said, "What do you mean 'Goodnight'?"

"Well, if you decide to go to church, let me know because any woman that I'm going to be with has to go to church. That is what our life is going to be centered around. I will call you tomorrow. Before you go to bed, pray."

I went to church with my friend Brandy first. Then the next Saturday, Brandy and I were sitting in my apartment when I jumped up off my couch. She said, "What are you doing?" I said, "I have to go to church tomorrow!" I hadn't even thought about it or said anything to Jarvis. On Sunday, when he walked into church, I was already there. He said, "I didn't know you were coming." I said, "I didn't either." We've been going to church together ever since that day. I got baptized at a church picnic, and the kids were there with me. He could not go, but after we got married, we were baptized together.

Jarvis—I live by 2 Corinthians 5:17. It says, "If anyone is in Christ, the new creation has come: the old has gone, the new is here!" I preach that to people all the time because anyone can be born again. Jeremiah 29:11 is also a favorite. It says, "I know the plans I have for you."

Connie—Being a cancer survivor really changes your outlook on life. I have had breast cancer five times. The last time they said they refused to give me any treatment unless I really wanted to because there was nothing they could do.

Jarvis—She was bawling, and I said, "Nope, come home; don't worry about what man has told you because that is not what I am getting from God's Holy Spirit."

Connie—So he took me home to see my kids. Both of my sons' wives were pregnant at the time, and they said to me, "You have to be here when they are born. Do whatever you have to do to be here." I called my doctor and said, "I have to at least try treatment."

I went in for tests and completed four treatments to try and shrink the mass so they could do my surgery. Three days before my surgery I went in to do blood work. Everything was gone. Before treatment, you could see the knots in my back where the cancer was. A week and a half before my surgery the women at church touched me and prayed. A woman who was a breast cancer survivor and had her breast removed put her hands on the knot, and then all the women of the church surrounded me and prayed.

The doctor came in after the tests and said, "Connie, I'm confused."

I said, "Why?"

"Well, your doctor is not here so I'm just going to wait, and he will be in tomorrow and call you."

I said, "No, you need to tell me now."

Jarvis could not get off work, so I was all alone and was just terrified. I was afraid they were going to tell me they could do absolutely nothing and it was worse than before. He said, "I don't see anything on your tests, and I think they mixed your test up with somebody else's. I don't know what to tell you; you have to wait for your doctor."

I said, "That is not what is wrong. You don't see anything on my test, and you won't tell me that because you are a doctor and you want to be some big miracle medical worker and you know it is God and you will not say it."

Jarvis—Let me put a twist on this story for you. Prior to the praying that went on and the surgery she was going to have, one day without her knowing, I did something that really made me see the power of prayer. Two of my sisters also had cancer. All three of them were battling cancer at the same exact time: one sister with breast cancer and the other with colon cancer. So I had this load on my shoulders. I could be losing three people in my life at the same time. I was breaking down. Sitting on the side of my bed, I got down on my knees and said, "Lord, if this be Your will, take this from them and place it on me."

Connie and both of my sisters are going to be okay. (One is still battling cancer and in remission, but she is fine). Let me tell you how I know God hears my prayers and to watch what you pray for. Two months later I go in to see my doctor because I'm having trouble breathing. They do tests and X-rays over my chest, and they find a spot on my right lung and say they need to check that out. They did further testing, and the doctor came in with this bewildered look on her face and said, "We're going to send you to Iowa City to the cancer center. You need to go immediately." I couldn't believe it. The doctor looked at me, patted me on the back, and said, "Go and enjoy your family because you have a fight on your hands, and there is probably nothing we can do for you." That was the same thing they told my wife. When I got to Iowa City, they did the tests they needed to do. We came back and the church prayed. We were crying. We saw the X-rays and the spot. It was big. I could actually feel it and coughed all the time.

I fell back on relying on the Word of God. I turned to James 5:11-15 where it says, "Call on the elders of the church to pray over you and anoint you with oil and you will be healed." I live by that Scripture, that chapter in the Bible. The four elders of the church touched me, prayed for me, and anointed me with oil just like the Bible says. Then Iowa City called me and said, "You need to get up here. We need to discuss some things." I thought, *Okay, we are making my death plan, treatments, etc.* When I got there, the doctor came in and said, "Do you know why you are here?"

I said, "Yes, I have cancer."

All the screens were up, and she showed me the before X-ray and then the X-ray of a more recent scan. As sure as I'm sitting here, it looked like two different people. The second scan was completely clear. That doctor looked at me and said, "I can't explain it. I don't know what happened."

I said, "Oh, but I do."

"We didn't find any infection in your blood, no virus, nothing in you."

I said, "Wow, you doctors rely on science, but I rely on God and the Word of God, and I live by the Scripture."

Before I found out about my clean health results, I continued to go into Bridges and pray for those guys. I never skipped a beat or stopped for one minute praising God and doing God's work. One young man I was mentoring said, "Jarvis, why are you here praying for us and helping us when they told you they don't even know how long you have to live?"

I said, "Because my job never stops for God." That young man looked at me with tears in his eyes and could not believe that my job for God would never stop, no matter what.

I announced my testimony at a Bridges graduation. When I announced that the cancer was all gone and the doctors found nothing, the place just lit up. God said, *I'm going to take this away from you, but I want you to give this testimony and let people know that I am still working miracles.* To this day, He is still working miracles. We have documents to show that disease was there. They declared it, and yet today we sit here.

Right now I'm starting up a ministry called The Joshua Tree Ministry based on our last name. I'm trying to get it up and running because we already go out and help the homeless, especially in the wintertime. We gather up coats, blankets, and food and then get out into the field and help people. My goal is to just go out wherever God leads me. I am a follower of Christ, a true follower, and I've preached that sermon before. So many Christians claim they are followers of Jesus Christ. If you are a follower, then get behind Him and don't try to get in front of Him because then you will start trying to do your own will. If you are a true follower of Jesus Christ, you will stand behind Him and follow His lead, wherever He leads.

Kevin

It is my hope that I can provide some kindling, logs, or even a spark to your already burning or recently extinguished spiritual fires. Even though we're all at different points in our own unique faith journey, God calls us to share because, whether we recognize it or not, or whether we care to admit it, He is a huge part of the voyage. By sharing my story, I hope that you see not me but only Him. I want to tell you about my life, about growing up in a family that never attended a church or sought community, and how that all changed through the beautiful grace of God.

When I was a kid, I felt like a victim. By the time I was a preteen, I was very bitter and troubled. I disobeyed my parents frequently and did many disrespectful things. As a student I was an anomaly. I was a kid who got near perfect ITBS scores and great grades and participated in talented and gifted programs but got suspensions a couple times a year and caused many disruptions during classes. Despite my transgressions, teachers still poured into me. A teacher from the TAG program gave me a computer when I was around ten. I remember using the computer for games like Oregon Trail. I was so frustrated and sickened when I came home a couple weeks later to see that my computer and bike were missing. My mom's friend stole them and pawned them off (or so she told me). I felt like I was doomed. I couldn't get ahead and didn't feel loved. That's when I fell into bad habits on the weekends. This was around the age of thirteen. That lasted until I was seventeen.

Around the start of my junior year of high school, a beautiful girl in my school came up and asked me to join the cross-country team. The team was one guy short of having a full roster. I'm so glad I wanted to impress that girl. She's the woman who changed my perspective, opened me up to God, and changed my life. I saw a potential future with this girl, whom I started dating, and wanted to make that a reality. I changed for the better.

In college I finally had the exposure to Christ that I was ready for. I auditioned for a vocal music scholarship and was awarded a spot in the Wartburg choir. My wife and I both sang in that choir for the four years at Wartburg. During a performance overseas, God's love finally hit me. We were singing our first concert when all His grace flooded my soul. We were singing Psalm 23, "The Lord Is My Shepherd." During that song, my life flashed before my eyes, and I began to weep. As I wept, I felt the biggest, warmest hands in the universe envelop my body. It was the most supernatural experience I ever had. I was floored with God's love. Soon thereafter, I went through an adult communion class and was baptized. I've been attempting Christianity ever since.

As I reflect on a few of these stories, I've neglected the importance of music in my life. Music is how God first touched my heart. I worship God in song almost every single day—before I come to work and after work. Singing is my favorite way to pray. One of my favorite songs talks of the tough times and how God's love is a beacon of light through the dark. The song is called "My Lighthouse."

Over the past few years, I've come to know Christ personally through prayer, worship, and reflection over Scripture. God calls us to come closer to Him so that He can fix us up and make us new. It's up to us to hold up our end of the bargain.

My marriage has been amazing. My wife, Lexi, is the most wonderful person and draws me closer to God each day. Things like praying together, singing together, and sharing friendships have drawn us closer to each other and to God. I've always felt like we're a team and that our partnership is fortified more and more when we continually seek Christ. Is it always easy? No. Do we have the consistency we could have when it comes to seeking out the Lord? I don't think so. We are certainly a work in progress. But that's not a condemnation. On the contrary, that is a point of excitement. God has bigger plans for our marriage than either of us does, and that excites us both.

Shawn

I was born in North Carolina, but my dad was in the military so we moved around quite a bit. When I was growing up, I thought I had two sisters, a mom, and a dad. Right before second grade, my mom and dad separated and divorced. One night I found out my two sisters were really my half-sisters, and it basically blew my mind. My mom told me I was going to go live with my dad, and the girls were going to live with somebody on the East Coast. The way I see it, I was abandoned. At that time, I hadn't been around my dad at all, and then he just came and picked me up.

My dad was from the Marines so he was very heavy-handed. There was a very heavy consequence for anything I would do. I've been beaten quite a bit. I kept rebelling against my dad, and finally, three or four years later, my mom came back around. She got my two sisters back, and we kind of rekindled a relationship. My dad was very upset about that. By then he had married another lady, and I had two stepbrothers and stepsisters who would get me high and smoke weed. In the early 1980s, from around the third through fifth grades, I was smoking weed and getting drunk.

By the time I was seventeen, my dad was still a heavy-hand, but I knew he couldn't do anything really. When I turned eighteen, some kids I ran with stole a camera, and I pawned it. I got caught with stolen property. So I was eighteen and had a felony charge. I got arrested, went out on pretrial release, and basically started running from there. From eighteen until twenty, I lived on the streets or at whoever's house I could stay. Through the whole thing, I was partying and having a good time.

Fast-forward to 2006. I'd been clean since 1998, but that year my future wife, Olivia, and I went to a bike rally and got some coke. The first time, we only did a little bit. Another bike rally came, and I got more. Then it just started evolving into a bigger problem. In August of 2006, I married Olivia. I thought I was a big dope man, still holding down a good job, buying this, selling that. Then it turned back into addiction, and it just went to hell. I got her involved with drugs again, I got involved with drugs, and my child and stepson were dealing with addiction.

I admitted to myself, *I'm going downhill. I want to give her back to her mom.* Finally, my wife said, "I can't do it anymore." I remember looking at her and saying, "We aren't going to get clean together. We have to do something." We separated for a while, and I was hell-bound. I thought, *I'll go to prison, and I'll get clean again. Things will work out.* That was my mentality: *I'll just keep doing what I'm doing until I get caught and go to prison. Then I'll get clean and walk out as a new man.*

That didn't work. I did get caught. I was trying to make meth, so we were stealing anhydrous, and I got on a little high-speed chase. I got rid of all that stuff, but they found a little piece of crack cocaine in my car. Because of all my drug convictions, they used that little piece to charge me with a Class D felony, and that's five years' jail time. I was running on the streets again and doing what I knew how to do. My house got foreclosed on. I lost my job. Everything started falling apart because of drugs.

I went to court, and they gave me probation. The day I got sentenced, my wife filed papers on me for a divorce. All this happened at once. On Christmas Eve of 2008, I was supposed to go see my parole officer, and I knew I wasn't clean. I told her I couldn't go to the bathroom, so I sat there for like eight hours. I had to go to the bathroom so bad. She's said, "Alright, well, you need to come back in three days." I thought, *In three days, I can be clean.* But I couldn't do it. As soon as I left there, I got high. When I did go back, I dropped a dirty urinalysis and then ran. They put a warrant out for me. This was March of 2009.

Through this whole ordeal, I had my house. They had foreclosed on it, but I was basically living in an abandoned house—no power, no water, just a place I could go hide. Two weeks went by and no one found me. There was a mezzanine in the house, and I had an extension cord. I remember tying the extension cord up to hang myself. I thought, *When I wake up, I'll do it.* But when I woke up, I made a vow to myself. I said to myself, *Hey, you're going to turn yourself in. You're going to go to in-jail treatment, and you're going to go to this program.* (I didn't know what the program was, but it turned out to be Bridges.) So that's what I did. I turned myself in, and they arrested me.

That first month in Polk County Jail, a man named Jerry came up to me and said, "Is your name Shawn?" I said, "Yes." He said, "Do you want to talk to me?" He carried a Bible. I was confused and said, "What?" He said, "Well, somehow I've got a note in here saying you want to see me." I said, "I don't want to see you, but I'll hear what you have to say."

I knew about God, but I didn't know how to know Him better. I wasn't saved at the time. We went into a little room, and he started spewing answers to all these questions I had. I thought, *What's going on?* He said, "Do you want a Bible?" I said, "Sure, I'll take one."

I can't read, write, or spell very well. I can comprehend well if I hear it; I just can't do those other things well. He gave me a Bible and then said, "Come see me once or twice a week." I remember sitting in that room a week later telling him, "Hey, I read a chapter today." I felt proud.

I was given an option: I could go to prison or do in-jail treatment. There are two types of treatment. Sometimes they would bring a Bible study into our pods, and we would go into the TV room to be taught the Word as a group. Then there were individual meetings where they would put us in what is called a "lawyer room" to have discussions in private.

I was reading the Bible and learning about God from Jerry. One day I said, "You know, I just want to be saved." So we said the prayer, and in June 2009 I was saved.

While in jail, I met a guy who said, "You probably need to go to Bridges." Bridges is a halfway house. I had never heard of it, but I told my counselor I wanted to go to Bridges.

Justin (my cellmate in jail) and I bumped heads a lot. He was ahead of me on the list for Bridges, and they sent him there. My counselor wanted me to go somewhere else, even though I told him that was where I wanted to go. He said, "Nah, you probably won't get into Bridges." I called my aunt, who is a Christian, and said, "Hey, Aunt Valerie, call up Bridges and see what I can do to get in there." The door flew wide open. They came to visit me and agreed to let me join the program.

Remember, I was still saved, but just as raw as can be. I got out just after Labor Day weekend. I called my aunt and asked her to bring me some clothes for the graduation. She agreed. They had a little gray bus. I remember looking out the window and thinking, *I'm out, but I feel like I'm in a fish tank.* I went to the graduation, and everyone was teary-eyed.

At Bridges, phases one and two are sixty days each, and then the rest is phase three. Basically, phase one is just all treatment. You're in this little bubble. You can see outside, but you don't really get to move outside. It's just an "inside" treatment for sixty days. I have a work ethic, though, and I thought, *Man, I just need to get out and work.*

I still had a relationship with my aunt, but I had no relationship with my dad. I didn't want to deal with that stuff because I had disappointed him. I called my chaplain, Ken, and said, "Hey, last time I saw you, you said you were going to come visit me, and it's been thirty days." He said,

"I'll be right there." While we were talking, Ken asked, "How much are you into the Word? What church are you going to?" I was bouncing around and couldn't find a church. I would go here and there. He said, "Why don't you come to church with me?"

So every Sunday he would pick me up. Since he was on the board of directors, he could come and go as much as he wanted and pull whoever he wanted. So, even though I was in phase one, I could go to church with him. Then he said, "What about Bible study on Wednesday?" So I went to Bible study.

Through this whole ordeal I was saved, but like I said, I was just raw and didn't want to let go of anything. I was always getting into trouble. I was going to Bible study and kind of working it out, but not really getting it together. Then the sixty days were up, and I went job searching. In late 2008 or 2009, the economy was bad. I was on a job search for nine weeks in the middle of the winter, trying to get a job, but I couldn't find one. By then I was visiting my aunt and talking to my dad a little bit. One weekend, I was about ready to walk out. I was just done.

On December 19, I thought, *Forget it. I can't find a job. I can't do anything. It's just not working. I'm just going to go on the run.* I remember a counselor told me to just give it a weekend. I thought, *Okay, I surrender. Whatever You want me to do, God, I'll just do it.* So I called my dad that Saturday. By Monday he found me a job with one of his longtime customers. The guy was a Christian and super kindhearted. I was an animal, just raw and angry. He said, "What do you need?" I said, "I need forty hours, and I need you to do this. I need to be off at this time, and I need to do this." I was spitting out commands like crazy. He said, "No problem." I worked there for a couple months. Through this job, I was able to deal with people, and I'm not a "people" person, so it was really helping me.

I had to be at work at nine o'clock. But at Bridges you have to get up early and ride the bus. Sometimes while riding the bus, I would read Scripture out of a little sample Bible. If I was dealing with anger that day, I'd look up Bible verses in that Bible. I truly believe that's where the foundation of my relationship with God really came into effect. Ken would pick me up at Aurora Street and then take me to a place across the street from Bonanza. We would have coffee with some old guys. We would just sit and talk, and I felt normal. Then I would go across the street to work and eat at Bonanza. My boss never let employees take food home, but he would let me take food home. He was that kind of guy.

Later I decided I needed a better job, and I got one. I was still on probation. I had three charges: two for drugs and one because I didn't pay any of my fines or court costs. I started phase three on a Friday and went to court on Monday. My aunt went with me. The judge gave me two options: prison or pay. I had $1,200 in fees. He told me that if I paid, I could be off probation that day.

I looked at my aunt and said, "What do you want to do?" She said, "I'm paying it right now." So, on Friday, I went on phase three, and on Monday I wasn't on probation anymore. I wasn't held down to Bridges. I could have left that day, but I went back to Bridges and told them, "I'm off probation, but I want to stay and graduate from this program." They were happy to hear it. So I graduated from Bridges. Although it's a one-year program, they let me out in nine months. I'm still going to church and trying to get back to Bridges to help people. Whenever they want to come to church, I get them to church. I still have a relationship with Ken. Every Saturday I have breakfast with him and the old guys.

One of my buddies, Timmy, is a lineman, and he's way bigger than me. I thought, *Man, if he can do it, then I can do it!* I had the interview and didn't have a lick of experience. They do it in a ranking deal. I was forty-one years old at the time, and these kids were young—twenty-five or whatever. They slotted me in at number nine. That was hard to believe. It was all God! I got in, and they indentured me. I went to boot camp (it's basically four years of school). I can't read or write very well because of dyslexia. Remember this, though, I was reading the Bible. The Bible helped me to read, and it was helping me to write. It was helping me understand these words. It was maturing me for my next step.

Last month I finished all my schooling. I truly believe it was all God. Through this whole ordeal, God is changing my life, and He's molding me into what He wants me to be. I made it through there, and now I'm working. In 2009, I was making $8.25 an hour. Today I'm making $35.50. God is doing all of this.

My dad is an electrician as well. As I was growing up, and as I went through Bridges, I wanted to make my dad happy. If I did my dad wrong, it would be a bad situation. When I got saved, God became my Father. So instead of worrying about what my dad is thinking, all I've got to do is worry about what God is thinking. If I screw up with Him, He's going to give me consequences, but He still loves me no matter what I do. See what I'm saying? It's not a one-sided street, you know, like when it came to my dad.

As soon as I focused on making my Father happy, my dad became a friend. Now we have a relationship as friends. A cool part of it is that my dad was a lineman when he was my age, but it was a different style then. Now I'm kind of following in my dad's footsteps, and I've got a friend who has my back. That's my dad. He moved to Montana, but I still have a relationship with him. It's long distance, but it's good.

For years and years, I was a blooming, raging idiot. Can I still get that way today? Yes. When I let my flesh be in control. You would be surprised at how many people have told me they can see the change. That's a big deal to me. From the day I got arrested until now, it's been a transformation. But it's hard.

You need to care what God thinks. That's what keeps me in line—I fear God and what He's going to do. He could slap me with a hand, or He could just whack me right on the old head. I don't fear much; I've been shot, stabbed, in a motorcycle accident, and through the gates of hell. The only person or thing I fear is God.

I truly believe when it comes to addiction, or anything else, it's a spiritual battle. If you don't have a spiritual bank going on, you're going to deplete. You're going to take whatever you possibly can, just like the devil does. If you have a spiritual bank and have the Spirit, you can radiate that. When you have that spiritual bank, you are going to win the battles. You just have to be spiritual. The only way I know how to get it is through prayer and the Bible.

Robbie, Aaron, Beth, and Cody

Robbie – We serve a great God. When He grabs ahold of your heart, He reveals to you who He is and who you are. Then He begins to mold you into His identity. That transformation is just beautiful. The experience and the process you get to go through is overwhelming.

I'm thirty-five years old, and my experience with God humbling my heart has been completely personal. I've been through some terrible things, and I truly believe it's because God wanted me to grow into the man He has called me to be.

I grew up in the church and came from a poor family. We had a cultural belief while living in a black community that everything is set before you. You are either going to be living off the state for the rest of your life, or you are never going to amount to anything or have anything. In my household, my mom and dad were both alcoholics. My mom would beat us all the time, so I never really got to experience what love was truly like or see what love even looked like. As a child, my household was always dramatic—it was crazy. I went through a lot of abuse as a child, not only from my parents but from my older brother as well.

By the time I was fourteen, I was already into drugs heavily. I sold drugs, used drugs, and became a gangbanger. That gave me my sense of identity; that's who I was. I was naturally a leader, so it wasn't long before I was leading the gangs a lot. I was shooting a lot and got shot twice. I believed in my heart that by eighteen I would either be dead or in prison. That was just the destiny for me. I didn't know God had other plans.

By the time I was nineteen I ended up going to prison on an assault charge. My first experience with prison was not hard. When I got to prison, all my old homies that I didn't see on the streets anymore were there. It was like going back into the neighborhood, but segregated, big-time. It was easy to hook up with them. The nights were lonely and depressing because, at the end of the day, I still had to go in that cell. I would remember, reminisce, and think about all the pain and hurt.

It may sound odd, but I loved it because I found a sense of security in prison. I was accepted. I kept that same old demeanor. As soon as I got to the prison yard, I found the first guy and fought him just because I wanted people to know who I was. At the same time, while in prison I read the Bible from Genesis to Revelation six times. I didn't get anything from it. It was a whole bunch of crazy stories and words I couldn't even pronounce. I remember talking to an older gentleman, and he said, "You do not want to turn forty in prison." I didn't get what he was talking about. I thought, *I'm not going to be turning forty in here.* But it's a revolving door. If you don't start changing your life, this is where you are going to be over and over again. I did nine months, and then they discharged my sentence.

I was out of prison for nine months, and then I was back in prison with a seventy-two-year sentence. This time around I was accustomed to prison life and people knew who I was. I ended up going to this program called ICI (Inter-Change Initiative), a Christian-based program. Getting accepted into that program was God's divine intervention because I was not supposed to go to it. My mandatory was too long. Right before I went to the program, on July 3, 2002, my father passed away. I remember them calling me over and telling me about it. They said, "Your dad just passed. A truck fell on him and crushed his chest." I went back to my cell and told my "cellies." I was crying. I don't know who my real dad is, but the man who died was my father. I was weeping, and I thought, *I can't spend the rest of my life in prison. This cannot be my life. This cannot be it.* It felt like God was stirring something in me because I didn't want to bear this pain by myself.

Two weeks later, I started the program. I knew the condition of my heart at the time. The program felt right. It was different. The presence of the Holy Spirit was there, and I knew that, but I didn't understand who God was. On August 9, 2002, I was sitting in a revival, and a guy named Chris was leading the worship service. As I was sitting by myself, I kept having these heavy sensations in my heart. My heart kept beating faster and faster and harder and harder, and at that moment I felt this overwhelming feeling. I thought, *Get on your knees. Turn around, get on your knees, and put your face in the chair.* That is what I did. I said, "I give my life to You, Jesus. I believe You died on the cross for my sins. I believe You sat at the right hand of the Father, and You rose from the dead. Holy Spirit, I want You in my life."

That was my moment of salvation, when God saved me and saved my life. He called me at that moment. He chose me at that moment and gave me the heart to accept Him. I stood up, looked out, and knew everything was different. I didn't understand it, but things looked different. I felt pain for things that had happened in my life. I felt a lot of pain for the people I had hurt and the things I had done. However, I still was the same old guy. At this point, I didn't have any relationship with Jesus, by any means. I still was Robbie.

When people were around worshipping, I was like, "Hey, hallelujah, praise God!" I would sing the worship songs, but when the door closed and the counselor was out, I was playing cards and gambling again, talking trash and cussing. It was one of those things where I had a moment of clarity and where God saved my soul, but the transition had not happened yet. On October 29, 2003, they called me over and told me that my son had passed. He died in a house fire. He was five years old. That was the beginning of me seeing who Jesus was. I went back to my cell, and all the Christians who were in the program (242 men) began coming to that wing of the prison cell unit. They gathered around me and prayed over me. God began to take that burden from me. The pain hurt so bad because I felt so worthless. I was not a father, and I had never been there for him. I don't even remember a lot about that kid, but he was my son.

Earlier I had read a little pamphlet on prayer. At the end of the book, it said, "Write a prayer down and pray about it for thirty days in a row, and God will answer this prayer." So I wrote, "I want to be able to witness to all of my old friends that knew who I was from the past, and I want them to know that I am going to serve Jesus and that I love Jesus Christ." I wrote that and prayed that prayer. The thirtieth day was when my son passed away. I didn't put this together at the time.

I was blessed to go to his funeral, and I remember sitting there in the church with about four or five hundred people present. The pastor asked if anybody wanted to come up and say a few words. I kept feeling this tug like, *You need to go up there.* I kept thinking, *There is no way I'm going up there!*

I had shackles, handcuffs, and a belly chain on. I truly felt like Paul. Again, I had this thought, *You need to go up there.* I thought, *Man, Lord.* So I got up and began to walk forward across the front of the church. It was quiet, and they could hear me rattling probably miles away. As I walked past, I touched the casket where both my son and his younger brother (who was eighteen months old) were lying, both dead from the house fire. I prayed to the Holy Spirit, *Lord, I don't know what You want me to say. I have never been outspoken before, so You are going to have to do this. Anoint me to do Your will.* I went up and stood behind the pulpit. When I looked out, I remembered the prayer I wrote in that book. Everyone who knew who I was, those I ran with, who I gangbanged with, and my whole family were all sitting out there in that church. I asked my mom for forgiveness for the kind of son I was. I told my son's mom that I didn't blame her for what happened, that I should have been a father, and I should have been there for that boy. I should have done my part, but I chose prison and drugs. I chose that lifestyle over him. I repented. I spoke out and confessed that I gave my life to Jesus Christ and was going to serve Him with all my heart.

I felt God saying, "Somebody wants to give their life to Christ." I thought, *No way!* Again, God said, "Yes, somebody wants to give their life to Christ." So I said, "If anyone wants to know Jesus Christ, please stand." Ninety people stood and gave their lives to Christ—at my son's funeral!

I think about that moment to this day, and I don't really mourn tremendously over my son. I have wept. I have been bitter about him, but I remember that our pastor said one time, "A death is not a day of mourning, but a day of rejoicing." I knew my son did not die in vain. God had a purpose for that. I can't even imagine how many people know Christ today because of that one situation. I left the church that day a new man in Christ. My identity was completely changed at that moment. That was just the beginning of my walk.

After five years in prison, I entered back into society, the real world, where my faith really came to speak. I got out of prison on fire. I was in love with Jesus, but at the same time I had a lot of things in my flesh to deal with. I ended up getting married right away. My wife and I had terrible issues, and at one point I thought, *Okay, I'm going to try everything I can to save this marriage and make it work.* I read all the books. I did the counseling, but in my heart I still was not 100 percent sold out to it. I ended up committing adultery, getting a divorce, and losing the ministry I had with a best friend of mine. I remember standing in our house by myself. She had taken everything. I had nothing, and I was fine with that. I was at the lowest I could be. I told myself that drugs were not a choice and prison was not a choice. Surrendering to Jesus was the only choice I had. At that moment, I surrendered to God and said, "I don't know how I got here, but I hate it, and I love You. I just pray that You take ahold of my life."

At that moment, I got a phone call. I was working for Vermeer Corporation in Pella. I had left there on a nine-month leave for ministry work. Now they wanted me to come back. I got everything back. It was like I never left. Then I met Emily, who I am married to now. She is a God-given lady that I love to death. God began to bring healing in my life. He began to change my heart and to restore and reconcile my family. Then He blessed me with two boys. Transforming from being sold out to my addiction to being sold out to Jesus truly is just about surrendering and building a relationship with Christ. I am falling in love with Christ. My relationship with Jesus has to be more of a relationship than the one with my wife, period. I love her, and every day I try to do better for that lady by becoming the husband God wants me to be. I want her to see Christ in me. I don't want her to just see me as a husband. I want her and others to see me and say, "Robbie is a man of God." That surpasses everything else. That is the overall vision of my life.

After going through all this, I was led to The Way, where I met my mentor and pastor. I took a class at the church called Emersion Journey Leadership where I met Aaron. Aaron, at the time, was an undercover cop. For a long time, I had a hatred in my heart toward cops because of the lifestyle I lived and from growing up in a community where we couldn't stand cops, specifically white cops. Then Aaron, one of these guys, was across the table from me. Because I loved Jesus, I had to see past that in my heart. I can say he probably had the same vibe toward me at first, because you have that perception for a long time.

During that course, we got to know each other well and became great friends. God ended up giving us the same vision: to be able to give back to people who have struggled with addiction. I experienced it firsthand. I was that guy. God transformed my life, redeeming me and changing my identity. Through that, Discover Hope was formed. Our goal was to help people make a transition in their lives, to break those addictions and form a bond with Jesus Christ. We want to help them with the necessary resources to make that transition, as well as give them a support group.

It took us two and a half years to just step out in faith and say, "Okay, God, what do You want us to do?" We decided, *Okay, we've got to go. We've got to just step out and go.* So, in June of 2014, we stepped out in faith with Discover Hope, and it has been a blessing. We've had a little over one hundred people come through the door, and they have been able to hear about Jesus. About ten to twelve core members come every week, and in the last few weeks twenty to twenty-five people have been showing up. It's been amazing to see God work through the people there, and I have been able to give back as well.

My experience with Christ has been amazing. Where I'm at with God right now is to serve Him with my whole heart and be obedient to the vision He's given Aaron and me as partners in this ministry. We don't have any agenda. We just want to serve God and carry out His Great Commission. We want to tell people about Him so they can see the Truth. I want to be a living testimony. It's one thing to read the Word of God and hear a sermon, but it's another thing to relate to it and want to testify to people about Christ. Realizing that God can help you through problems makes hope alive. When I go back into that prison, it's all about reassuring the people that prison does not have to be the end for them. If I can be out of prison, free from drugs, and serving a holy God, it can be the same for everyone because we serve the same God. He is restoring and reconciling my life. He gave me a great family and is blessing me abundantly. I'm in a season of my life that is a pruning season. I'm seeing what God wants to do with the ministry.

I don't just love God anymore; it is past love now. I am in love with Him. When I talk about Him and see the things He has done in my life, I desire Him more and more.

Aaron – My father was a law enforcement officer, and if I screwed up, I was always more afraid of him than the law. He was strict, and I feared his discipline, but I knew he loved me.

My dad grew up with an alcoholic father. At fourteen years old, my dad would have to go to the bar to pick up his father because he had passed out. He was beaten severely during his dad's alcoholic rages, thus he made a decision not to drink because he didn't want to put me through the same things he had to endure. I am forever thankful for that. He has always been a good man, a man of integrity.

I minded my p's and q's and was a pretty good kid growing up. My parents sent me to church, but they never went. I was very involved in the church youth group in middle school and high school. Then I went off to college, and things totally changed. I never drank at all before this. I got accepted to the United States Naval Academy, and once at the Naval Academy I ended up being more interested in drinking, partying, and chasing girls than I was about the academic portion of it. It is one of those institutions where if you are not all in, you will not be successful. I ended up failing out of the Naval Academy academically and going to college at William Penn in Iowa to wrestle. I kept drinking and partying during that time, doing the same old things that got me kicked out of college before.

I got hired at the Jasper County Sheriff's Office as a deputy while I was going to school at William Penn and eventually quit school and worked full-time. I met my wife at a bar in Des Moines (she was friends with my sister), and we eventually started dating. I would go visit her at school on my days off. Even while dating my wife and being in law enforcement, I was still partying and drinking. I almost lost my job because of it when I got a ticket in Cedar Falls at my girlfriend's apartment during a party. At that point, I knew I was done with the drinking and partying. I had enough because it almost cost me my job.

At this time in my life, I was selfish and essentially a nonbeliever. I had walked away from God, ignoring everything I had learned about Him. When I was going through middle school and high school, I would open the Bible and read it, so I knew who He was. Scripturally, my youth group instilled some things in me. But I fell away from it and questioned a lot of things. I got to the point where I thought it was ridiculous that people could believe something out of a book that was two thousand years old. I didn't want to go to church because I didn't want a pastor telling me how to live my life. I wanted to live life according to what I wanted.

I don't have an exact moment where I can say I surrendered my life to Christ, but I believe I was saved when I was younger. I totally fell away at some point in college, but God brought me back in, and it was through my wife and the church that He did that. The Way teaches the Bible, God's Word. They don't bend the truth; as a result, the church has grown tremendously. People are serving with compassionate hearts and leading others to Jesus. It truly is a tremendous place, and God is using it to do wonderful things.

My wife ended up getting hired by the church as the office manager, and now she's in charge of the youth group. Soon she will be transitioning into a financial manager role. It's crazy how God prepared her for this role through her college education and previous work experience.

Early on, I would just go to church every now and then because I worked overnights and my schedule was an excuse not to go. As we got more involved in the church, and as our walk with Christ strengthened, the push to attend church on Sunday grew stronger. The push came from God, and now our week doesn't seem complete if we don't go to church.

As my walk strengthened so did my compassion to help people. When I worked in narcotics, I kept seeing people throw their lives away because of addiction, and it sparked something in me. When it comes to things like meth and opiates, the dope is more important than family, kids, jobs, and friends. I saw this happening, and I thought, *We need something in this community to help addicts.* Eventually I got into a church leadership course called Emerging Journey, and there was a guy named Robbie in the class. I knew a little bit about his background, and I was very skeptical of him because, in my line of work, we deal with the same people over and over again. As law enforcement officers, we get this jaded mindset or this belief that people do not change, so I thought it was just a matter of time before Robbie slipped up again.

Little did I know that God would use Robbie to transform my heart.

I knew his background, but I didn't know much about him. As time went on, I saw his love for Christ, and I realized people CAN change. It's always neat for me to hear his testimony because people are just like, "Wow, I never expected you to live that lifestyle: being shot at, being in a gang, selling dope." To see who he is now, nobody would believe that he lived that type of life. God has transformed him the same way he transformed my heart. I believe our unique relationship allows God to use us as symbols of hope for people.

On Easter Sunday, about three years ago, Robbie and I did a cardboard testimony together at our church. In front of the congregation, we wrote on a piece of cardboard what life was like before Christ. On the other side, we wrote what our lives were like after knowing Christ. I told Robbie that we needed to do this together because it would be powerful. Mine said, "Angry, cop, nonbeliever, hated criminals." Robbie's said, "Angry, criminal who hated cops." We flipped them over, not knowing what each other wrote, and they both said, "Brothers in Christ." We have been stuck together ever since then. I know there are people in my profession, a lot of whom I work closely with, who probably look down on me because of my relationship with Robbie (because of the way he used to be). I know there are gangbangers (former associates of Robbie's) who would have his head if they knew he associated with me. Their opinions won't stop us. It is amazing when you get to that point with Christ where it doesn't matter what others think because God has called you to do this. Robbie knows me for who I am; he knows my heart, and I know his heart.

Throughout Emerging Journey, Robbie and I started talking about Newton (Iowa), our community. Newton is known all around the Midwest as being a methamphetamine town. It's a problem here, but there were no faith-based programs, no Christ-centered programs here to help people with their addiction. I knew a little bit about Teen Challenge, which has an 86 percent success rate with those who complete the program. Most secular programs have a 40-60 percent success rate. The numbers say there is success in faith-based programs.

I dragged my feet starting up the program with Robbie, and finally he said, "It's time to go. It's time to do it." We took that step of faith and started Discover Hope 517. We met with the pastor a few times, and he said, "Don't get disappointed and don't be surprised if you only have one or two people there." We started the Discover Hope class and went for forty-five minutes every other Tuesday night. Within the first month, we switched to a one-hour class every Tuesday night. We averaged about eight to twelve people every time. God was humbling me through His ministry.

After we had been going for six to eight months, the whole Ferguson, Missouri, thing blew up. We saw all this negative publicity between blacks and whites, specifically black criminals or convicts and white law enforcement officers. I looked at Robbie and said, "Do you understand what is going on right now and how huge it is for us to be able to do this together?" It is only through Christ that we are able to do this. Robbie said, "Ha, ha, I never thought about that." The fact that Robbie was a black convicted felon and I was a white law enforcement officer never came across our minds before that because of our identity in Christ. We saw each other for who we are in Christ, not a skin color or a profession. Society tells us a black convicted felon and a white cop should hate each other. God is showing society something different.

Beth – I was born in a loving Christian family, and we went to church twice a week. My parents loved me. I was never abused. I was well-treated. I was blessed from the moment I entered the world. When I was ten, my mom died of cancer and my dad remarried; I lived life very much like Cinderella. For years, I was verbally abused by my stepmother and sexually abused by a stepbrother. I graduated high school, and that whole entire time I went to church every week. I knew God, and I had a relationship with Jesus, but just to a certain extent. I call living at home "my angry years" with my dad and stepmother.

Within forty-eight hours after I graduated from high school, I moved out of my house and moved in with my sister. I never went back home, and I went a few years without speaking to my dad. I was a little girl; he did not protect me, and he didn't understand that. How could he not? I was also angry with God, not just because my mom died, but because of the awful situation I was in when my dad remarried.

I now had a new life, and it was better when I left home, but then I got into this awful phase. I used marijuana and started to use methamphetamine in the early 1990s. My husband was working on the road, and a guy he knew introduced it to him. He brought it home. The first time I used, it took me. I thought, Wow! I like it! My husband wasn't addicted to it, but I was. While he was working on the road, I had two kids at home. Meth makes you awake all the time. I could keep up with everything I needed to do. In the early stages it was fun, but by the end I hated it and couldn't live without it. I used for a total of about four years. I ended up using needles, something I never thought I would do, especially since I grew up as a Christian going to church camp.

There was one particular day I think of a lot. I was driving around Des Moines going from gas station to gas station, shooting loads of dope into my arms. That day I asked God, "Please, help me! Please come into my life and get me out of this hell I'm living in!" I was the kind of user that, when my husband was home with the kids, I would leave and go use because I didn't want to be using around my kids. I wasn't stealing to use. I would front meth from a guy and sell what I had to pay for my own. That was my world.

Not long after that day of shooting dope into my arm, I was arrested and got charged with possession of methamphetamine. My family had me committed into a drug treatment center, and I lived there as an in-patient for eight weeks. I went through grief therapy with a Holocaust survivor who lost all his family in the Holocaust. He had me write a letter to my mom. She died in 1974. We did not talk about her after she passed away, so I never really dealt with her death. I just lived with this awful pain inside for years. For me, using drugs killed that pain. I didn't have to feel the pain of losing my mother, the pain of being verbally abused by my stepmother, or of being sexually abused by my stepbrother, or the pain of my dad not protecting me from those things. I got through treatment and grief therapy in March of 1999, and I have been clean ever since. I made it, and I feel so blessed to be one of the ones who made it out.

In 2010, my mom's last sibling passed away. I was so close to her siblings because they were that last piece of her. He went to The Way church, and at his funeral, Pastor Steve spoke and said, "Roxie wanted you all to have a relationship with Jesus." After I got sober in 1999, I gave my life back to Christ, but I didn't really feed that relationship with Him. Because it was Roxie's dream for all of us, I said to my sister that day, "Let's go to church here on Sunday." We did, and I've been going to The Way ever since.

A few years later, Discover Hope started. One day I stopped at the church office to talk to Pastor Steve and Tricia, the office manager (Aaron's wife). We got into a conversation, and I let out a little bit of my story about being in recovery for sixteen-plus years. Tricia said, "You have got to come to church on Saturday night. Aaron and Robbie are going to be speaking about Discover Hope." So I did. I came that Saturday night, and I heard them talk about their stories. Wow! I was in love with what Jesus had done in their lives. It reminded me so much of myself and my oldest brother, who was in law enforcement. When my sister called him to tell him that I was in jail for possession of methamphetamine, he was literally walking up on a meth lab at that time. He was probably my toughest critic. He was not very happy with me. Today I consider him my very best friend. Imagine that! That is one of the many things the Lord has done in my life.

So these guys spoke Saturday night at church. Then I got up Sunday morning and went to church because I had to hear it again. I was on fire for what they were doing, and God was calling me to be a part of Discover Hope because I know how hard it is to get clean. I know the struggles, and I know you have to have Jesus. You cannot do it alone. I see methamphetamine as the devil, and when you are messing with that stuff, it's the devil's playground. It's not the only drug that does that, but that is the one that took me.

I have been a part of Discover Hope since December 2014. Today my relationship with Jesus is stronger than it has ever been. I've gone through a lot of crap in my life. I've been able to forgive those people who did me wrong, mostly because I feel sorry for them; they caused so much pain to people, including me. I ended up feeling sorry for my dad and for the fact that he wasn't the dad he should have been to me. He died in 2008.

I have been blessed in so many ways. I have a beautiful family, a beautiful home, Christ is in my heart, and my marriage survived all of that. It was not all peaches and cream, but the Lord gave me a wonderful husband. I look for the good in everyone, regardless of the choices they make, and that is a blessing. I have a son who is like Robbie and a son who is like Aaron, and somehow I balance it.

Cody – I'm a recovering alcoholic, but through the power of Christ, the fellowship of men and women in recovery, and excellent leadership, I haven't found the need to take a drink since February 28, 2013, and for that I am truly grateful.

I was a pretty good kid growing up. I played sports, hung out with friends, and did the normal things that kids do. I wasn't the greatest student, but I did enough to get by. I was smaller than everybody else, the runt of the litter, I guess, so that naturally led me to be a bit timid. I was also a very polite but shy child. I spoke when spoken to and never really branched out or took the lead in anything that was presented to me.

Being the smaller kid, I got picked on a lot. That led me to be a bit of a hothead, and, quite frankly, I just took myself too seriously. I never really learned to laugh at myself or my mistakes.

I think I always knew there was a God, but I never felt that He had any time for me. I just felt too ordinary. My mother grew up Catholic but was kicked out of the church because of pregnancy out of wedlock and an abortion. Because of that, she seemed to harbor resentment toward religion. My father, on the other hand, had a little more of a grassroots approach toward God. He has always believed in God, but also had his own beliefs about God. From my knowledge, his side of the family didn't really attend church or claim to be practicing Christians. So, when it came to us kids, we were shown church and told that it was an option for us, but we never really attended. I can remember thinking, *Why would I go to church when I could be outside playing or watching football?*

I was first introduced to alcohol after graduation. Beer just wasn't my thing, so I was smoking a little weed and casually drinking liquor on the weekends. I was the life of the party! Suddenly, I could talk to girls without clamming up. I was able to do things I didn't have the nerve to do when I was sober. I prided myself on being a "weekend warrior." The good times didn't last long, though. Within a couple of years, I was drinking three to four nights a week.

Eventually I met a girl. I knew in my heart that things were going to change for me. I loved her. I wanted to spend the rest of my life with her. But little did I know my drinking had caught up to me. I had no clue that those demons had already taken hold of me. I worked mornings while she worked evenings, so every once in a while she would come home and I would be passed out drunk or so intoxicated she couldn't stand to be around me. This lasted for a while until she couldn't take any more of it. She grew cold. I had hurt her too many times. Some scars just don't heal, and some things that are broken cannot be repaired. This was the first, but certainly not the last, failure that happened to me while I was actively drinking.

I had a hard time dealing with the breakup of that relationship. My drinking had certainly gotten out of control. Growing up, I never learned proper ways to deal with my emotions. Lashing out in some way or form was all I knew. Alcohol was the perfect release. I didn't have to think about those failures or those emotions.

Soon after the breakup, I was arrested for my first OWI. Due to having no home and the consequences of that OWI, I moved in with my parents that week. The following weekend, I picked up a second OWI. I went through the process and received five days in jail and a year of probation. I had never been to jail. This wasn't my fault. Everyone but me was to blame.

I kept that mentality for years. I gave myself every reason to drink. When things went good, I drank. When things went bad, I drank. You get the picture? That inward thinking had led me to isolation, a family that had given up on me, friends who didn't want to be around me any longer, four more OWIs, more jail time, and eventually prison.

Prison was a relief! That sounds crazy, but I knew it was the one place where the disease couldn't touch me. It was sanctuary. I was confined, but free to be me again. I was finally able to be somewhat honest with myself. It was also the first time I had the courage to explain who I was to my current fiancée, Katie. We had been friends for a few years. Secretly, I knew it could be more than that. I wouldn't allow it, though. The drinking was too much, and I didn't want to ruin her. It's funny because my mother had always asked me when I was going to start dating again or when I was going to settle down, and I would always tell her, "If Katie didn't live in Newton, I would." Amazingly enough, she stuck around. Who would have thought? I ended up doing most of my time in the Newton CRC, so she came to visit me three days a week. Our bond just grew stronger. Even though I was in prison, things were actually looking up for me. Coincidentally, it was also the longest I had been sober in my adult life.

I managed to stay sober for about four months before I ended up bellying up to the bar after a shift. On October 1, 2012, my son was born. I had it all. I had the job, the girlfriend, the baby, and the house. We could grow. Unfortunately, nothing grows in the dark. I still hadn't taken a look at myself and the reasons why I drank. Things went from bad to worse, and eventually I found myself on the outside of my family, looking in. I still had the job, and I rented an apartment down the street. I was nonexistent in my son's life, and Katie couldn't depend on me. I barely made it to work every day, and in the evenings I was off to the races, drinking and chasing women.

One morning I woke up in an empty apartment with a mostly cashed bottle of rum next to the bed, and I couldn't move. I had always just assumed I would go to heaven. It was never a question. If you believed, then you go. I had the worst hangover of my life. I finally got out of bed, or fell out, if you will. Luckily, my knees broke my fall. I cried out. I just couldn't do it anymore. I couldn't continue to live like that. I yelled at a

God I knew nothing about. I gave HIM a choice: take my life or help me. For the longest time, I had no explanation for what happened next. A tiny voice in my head said, *Well, what are you going to do?* It was the first time in a long time that I had been presented a choice. I could instantly evaluate and think clearly. Something had to be done. Alcohol was a handcuff, and in time I learned that Jesus was the key. I instantly called my parole officer. I had a plan. I confessed everything to her. I told her about all the drinking. I also told her that I was going to place myself in treatment.

I spoke with the House of Mercy. They set me up with a twenty-eight-day stay at Prairie Ridge in Mason City. I called Katie and informed her of my plan. I called my boss, filled out the paperwork, and took a leave of absence from work. Within two days, I was in Mason City. I didn't have to detox. I didn't have to spend a few days in a hospital. All the obsession and all the physical craving had been taken from me. In treatment, I came to see my love for helping others like me. I was introduced to a 12-step program. The program taught me that all I had to do to stay sober was believe in a higher power of my understanding. Coming from no spiritual background, that was something I could grasp ahold of.

Twenty-eight days later, I was released from treatment and came back to Newton. I immediately got involved in a 12-step program. Through that program, I was able to break down sobriety into small bites, rather than an entire meal. I got a sponsor, and together we looked at the things that were holding me back from a happy, sober life. We also explored just who my higher power was. I knew I was powerless over alcohol and that my life had become unmanageable. I had come to believe that a higher power of my understanding could restore me to sanity, and I was willing to turn my will and life over to Him. I just didn't know who He was.

It was around that time that Katie decided to start church shopping and found The Way. I was a bit hesitant to start going to church. I had all these preconceived notions in my head about organized religion. She went to Sunday service one day and came back elated. She begged and pleaded for me to come with her, saying that The Way was unlike any other church and that if anybody could feel at home there it would be me. I had learned that I needed to keep an open mind if I wanted to keep my sobriety, so I decided to check it out.

That first Sunday service was amazing! The pastor wore sandals, which basically broke every stigma I had about church. I knew right then that I had to go back. I had found a home. I opened the handout given to me and saw an ad for Discover Hope 517. It was for people like me. I could go there and explore God and get to know Jesus in a comfortable environment. It was exactly what I needed.

Through Discover Hope, The Way, and the 12-step program, I've been able to not only discover who I am but also discover little bits of who Jesus is and how I fit into His plan. My hope for Discover Hope is that they continue to grow and thrive in the community and help those who are in the dark places of life. The world needs a flashlight to light the way out of addiction and into salvation, and I feel like Discover Hope can be just that.

My God is such an amazing, awesome God. He has given me a life I never would have imagined for myself. I have finally grown up. I am the man—soon to be husband, father, brother, son, and friend—that I always wanted to be, but never knew how to be. To know that God gave His only living Son so that I can be forgiven of ALL the sins I have committed inspires me to be something positive in a troubled world. Being a man of Christ is the greatest gift I can ever give to the God who gave so much for me when I didn't deserve it. He has taught me humility and, above all, the true meaning of grace. Christ Jesus is my salvation. The Holy Spirit filled the void that needed to be filled my whole life. All I had to do was seek Him.

CHAPTER 2

Survivor

Whether facing an illness, serving in the military, or being held at gunpoint, these individuals learned they could not control the situation they were in. The only thing they could do was trust and depend on the Lord.

"Consider it pure joy, my brothers and sisters, whenever you face trials of many kinds, because you know that the testing of your faith produces perseverance. Let perseverance finish its work so that you may be mature and complete, not lacking anything."

James 1:2-4

Dave and Joan

Dave – God is my rock and my foundation. I have moments where I wonder about that, yet in the core of my being I know God is in control. I try to be content with that. That explains my philosophy in life; He is my rock, and God is God no matter what. He delighted in creating us. God is not there for us; instead, we are there for God. I try to live by that day by day. Fortunately, Joan and I see eye-to-eye on a lot of things regarding God, so raising our children with a united understanding has helped us fulfill our obligations toward our birth children and adopted children. As a couple, we have been able to bless our kids, and in turn we have been blessed big-time.

Has He always been my rock? I had a lot of rebellious years. Maybe it was because of the time period I grew up in. There was a lot going on, and I was a part of all that. I knew deep down that God was my foundation, though. I am now sixty years old and question myself. *Have I done everything I could to glorify God? Have I wasted my life?* No. There are things I could've done differently, but overall God has cared for us. We are very thankful for that.

There was a time in Guatemala that was the epitome of God. Not a day goes by that I don't think about it. God was right there when my nose was in the soil of Guatemala, with a machine gun sitting on my ear. It still brings tears to my eyes after twenty years. His presence was known. I went there for missionary work with my teenage daughter. A group of us were driving, and suddenly several men with guns took us and led us to a deserted place. We didn't know what they were going to do with us, and I feared for my teenage daughter. At one point, we all began praying together. Our heads were down, and then all the men just walked away with their guns. Several years later, our daughter wrote a paper in college about the experience. She titled it "My Two Fathers." She talked about how I was on top of her keeping her physically safe, and God was there protecting her from evil.

Joan – I always knew the Lord was watching over me. I have always been a Christian, but I guess it really hit me when we started going to a church where there were several adults who were new Christians. One individual wasn't a Christian until after she was married, but she was so pumped for the Lord. I thought, *Gosh, I'm not that excited for the Lord, but I could be.* She was thankful for everything in her life. That opened my mind up a lot.

I went to a conference with my oldest daughter, and I saw some kids that were fourteen, fifteen, and sixteen. They were so pumped for the Lord. I felt like I was missing out. *Why am I not feeling this way?* I wanted to change and became more excited for the Lord by studying the Bible more. I find myself going to Bible studies because I need them to get into the Word.

Sometimes I feel like I'm missing out because I want to share about God, but I am very hesitant about it. We just met some people recently. I wanted to ask if they knew God, but I didn't. I don't want to force it on anybody, but I want to open up about what the Lord has done for me.

I feel so blessed. I have a husband of thirty-seven years, and we have really clicked. We see eye-to-eye on so many things. If we don't, we work together until we do.

Throughout my life, I have not known a lot about the Bible, but my husband has helped me through this. He often says to me, "You don't have to know all the people's names. You just have to have it in your heart and know that the Lord saved us. Jesus died for us." I am so thankful he reminds me that you do not have to know everything.

God has blessed us through and through, and it is such a comfort. We are always learning about God and forever will be.

Bryan and Gail

Gail – Bryan and I are very different people. We met in high school and started dating at sixteen. We were married at nineteen and have been married now for over forty years, but we don't agree on almost anything. We are so incompatible it should not work. These last two years we battled cancer together. I was diagnosed with breast cancer. I think it strengthened our relationship in each other and in God. But we have been through very difficult times in marriage and in our relationship. I'm sure a lot of nonbelievers would have given up, and they would have missed the blessing. I think it's so sad when you see "empty nesters" out to eat and one is looking out the window while the other is watching people, or both are on their phones and there is no connection. They don't talk or even look at each other. I am NOT going to do that.

Bryan – Gail and I were pulled into some very difficult circumstances from outside our home. These circumstances and struggles often placed additional pressures on our marriage. Back then, I listened every morning to Dr. James Dobson on the radio, and one thing I learned is that the struggles in our marriage were common with other marriages. I also remember him saying that if you have big disagreements and you don't say anything, that means you don't really care. If you get upset and say something, it usually means there's a spark of intensity. God could have made it so we understand each other—men and women—but He didn't. There's got to be some humor in that. It's a lifelong learning process. Even if I don't understand, the longer we are married, the more I learn. The commitment has to be there. You have to find things to do together and allow God to be the center of the relationship.

I watched her go through the cancer trial, and her faith stayed strong as her health grew weak. I found out what it meant to be in the caretaker's role. Because of the opportunities, we both were able to show our faith and to witness.

Gail – (pulls out her phone) This is a photograph of pink roses blooming by my front door. I had been struggling with hot flashes and was going in to do a hormone check. In order to have the test, I had to have a mammogram done. That morning before the appointment, I was sitting in a chair on my front porch. I didn't want to go. I wanted to just sit and look at my roses that were starting to bloom. But I went and they found something right away. I could tell by the way they reacted. The first radiologist said there was something there, and then a second radiologist offered to do a biopsy on it immediately. She fit me in over her lunch hour, so I knew by their reactions that it was not good.

All weekend long, while I was waiting for the results, those roses kept popping up. I have such a special love for roses, and we had struggled with getting those roses to bloom. But while waiting from Friday until Monday to find out exactly what we were dealing with, those roses were constantly blooming. There were probably a thousand of them. The picture shows only one side of the door. We had the same amount on the other side.

I knew something bad was coming. Right after the biopsy, the radiologist said it was "doable." When I got a call on Monday confirming that what they found was cancer, the first thing she said to me was, "It is *still* doable." But it turned out to be a small subset of breast cancer isolated in 2006 that has a high tendency to come back and travel to other organs. This one was the kind where you have one shot at it, and, if it comes back, there aren't a lot of other options. But the roses were there, and they just kept coming and coming. It was like God was saying, "There is a trial coming, but look what I just did for you. If I can do this for you, look what else I can do for you." We are very grateful for the whole thing, even the bad stuff.

They caught it very early on. It was so small they could go in and remove it. They wanted me to get into chemo and radiation right away. My faith was really tested in figuring out how bad it was. On one hand, I thought, *Why me?* But then balancing on the other side were the roses and God saying, "This is happening to you, but I am walking with you."

Rick Warren said when he wrote *The Purpose Driven Life* that he used to think life was sometimes highs and sometimes lows, that your faith went up and down. But just when his book came out and made such an impact, his wife got the news that she had cancer. They were dealing with this huge success and blessing, and at the same time they were dealing with this devastating news and the struggle with her health. We know that we serve a good God but live in a broken world, and often the good and the bad are happening at the exact same time. We all have to make our decisions and our choices knowing that.

In some ways, it was harder on Bryan than on me. I would not have given it up, though, learning what we did from the experience. The two years we had to deal with my cancer solidified and clarified things for me. I didn't have any hair, and everybody recognized the hats. They could see there was something a little funky. People would just start conversations with me randomly—in the grocery line, at the YMCA, in Hobby Lobby. I was standing in Hobby Lobby, and a guy walked up to me and said, "You have cancer?" I said, "Yes." He had cancer too and was just losing his hair but hadn't shaved the rest yet. If someone told me I was going to have a conversation with a random stranger in Hobby Lobby, I would not have gone there. I would have said no (the nature of being an introvert). But that happened over and over again. A friend gave me a necklace that has little pendants with *courage, trust, strength*, an anchor, and a cross on it. I wore that every day, and I had people who looked at the hat and then at the necklace and then started conversations with me. It was almost a daily occurrence, and it always led to conversations about faith. I would tell people that cancer was a hard thing, but I was getting many blessings out of it.

I learned that I don't need to say anything to communicate Christ's love to others. Years ago I was asked to be part of a group in our church that went out to people's homes and knocked on doors to witness. I could pray for them but never could bring myself to actually go knock on doors like that. Those two years of cancer made it clear to me that, for me, that was not the way to go. God has His own way to make Himself known. I just opened myself up to ask, "Okay, God, where do I go with this?" It was completely natural. Some people reacted with a smile and responded with their own faith story. Some just smiled and didn't really understand, but that wasn't my responsibility, either. God would take it from there if that was His plan.

I keep reminding myself that this is all temporary. I think of the song *Every blessing You pour out I'll turn back to praise. When the darkness closes in, Lord, still I will say: Blessed be the Name of the Lord. Blessed be His glorious Name.* I have to continually remind myself, *You are feeling good and you are happy*, but that same phrase has to be applied even if I get the bad news someday. It could very well happen. I ask the ladies in my Bible study to pray that my testimony will hold, that it will stay strong and be happy and vibrant, even if something goes bad.

Darin and Tammy

Tammy – I gave my life to Christ when I was in school. When I married, I turned my back on God, but He never turned His back on me. My marriage of nine years was very rough. I kept thinking, *He will change. He will change.* People often told me that I could do so much better. All through this marriage I had a feeling way deep inside that something was going to happen. I didn't know what, but there was going to be a huge knock-down drag-out fight or something.

My ex went into business with a partner, and after a while that partner sat me down and said, "Tammy, let me tell you what this guy is doing to you." I thought, *Yeah, he's right.* Friends and family tried to warn me. I didn't listen because I thought he was going to change, but he never did.

One night I asked him, "What are your exact feelings for me?" He said, "Well, you know, you could have done a lot worse. You could have married somebody and lived on Sixth Avenue" (a scary part of town). I said, "That means this marriage is over." Looking back, he was very controlling and mentally and verbally abusive for nine years. So I left.

I started visiting the church where my mom and dad were going, and eventually I recommitted my life to Christ. Ever since then, I have learned more about Him by going to Sunday school and through relationships with the people at church. I met my husband, Darin, there.

Through my relationship with Christ, I learned that the feeling I had about my first husband was the Holy Spirit telling me, *This is not where you are supposed to be.* At that time, I had no clue what that was, but now I know. When He closes the door, He always opens a window. It might not be the window you want open, but it does open. I know that He is always with me and guiding me.

While going through those nine years of marriage, I thought I could only depend on myself. You can't do that. That's why God put everybody here: so we can all depend on each other. His Word says that we are to care for each other, help lift one another's burdens, and enjoy the good times with each other. Proverbs 11:14 says, "For lack of guidance a nation falls, but victory is won through many advisors." When Dad passed away everybody came up to me and said, "What can we do to help?" People helped with the garage sale, and I was so grateful for that.

When I was diagnosed with ovarian cancer, my sister-in-law, Judy, was in shock because I was so peaceful about it. I thought, *I have ovarian cancer. Okay.* One morning when I was driving to work, the sun just seemed to be a little brighter. The snow was whiter than normal. I was going across a river, and the mist was rising off the river and the colors seemed brighter. It was the strangest feeling. I found myself saying, "Thank You for that, Lord." We came to find out after everything was sent off to the lab that there was no ovarian cancer. Even though everyone around me was going nuts because I had ovarian cancer, I had this peace; the peace was God saying, *It's going to be okay, My child.*

Darin – I blamed God big-time when I got diagnosed with kidney trouble at seventeen: polycystic kidney disease, little cysts and polyps, kidney stones. Back then I thought, *I am invincible and nothing can happen to me. I've got one hundred years to live, and I can do anything.* Then I find this out at seventeen. Now I'm fifty and need a transplant. If I had a kid, he would've had a 70 percent chance of getting what I have. If we had two, the percentage went up, and I just couldn't do that.

It took me a long time to make peace with God. I never knew what healthy felt like. Most of the time doctors don't find the disease because it doesn't make you feel any different. So a lot of people die from it because they don't know. I was lucky they found it. I was at my sister's basketball game, and when I went to the bathroom I urinated blood. I thought, *Oh, crap, something is wrong!* We went to the doctor the next day. They ran tests and pretty much said I was kind of screwed. This hospital has been a big part of my life for a long time. I should be dead actually.

I did more yelling at God in this place than anywhere else. There were so many times I wanted to die. When I had a virus, it was the worst pain I've ever gone through in my life, and I just wanted to die in peace. I was angry at God for allowing this to happen to me. I didn't know why God was letting all this crap happen to both of us. It seemed like when something went right, something else would go wrong. This is how it was for four years. I thought, *Does God have it in for us or what?* It feels like it sometimes, and it stretches my faith, but I could not imagine going through it all without Him.

Matt

I worked at a summer church camp before joining the military. Once I joined, I got into contact with a military ministry called the Navigators. They helped shape me into who I am today. At one point, I was away from the states for two years; I spent eighteen months in Japan before I came home on leave, and then I went back for six more months then transferred to San Diego. All that time, I tried to stay in contact with the Navigators as much as I could. While in Japan, I got into contact with a missionary family there, and they welcomed me into their home. On Sundays, I attended a local church in the Japanese community where the missionary was the pastor. It was very eye-opening to see a Baptist church in the middle of a Japanese community. A lot of the locals attended. The common religion was Buddhism. Along the little roads in the small towns, you would see a lot of shrines to Buddha.

At one point, I wanted to get out of the Navy because I was homesick. I didn't know what to do, so I talked to the chaplain about trying to get out. Having worked at a church camp and then with the Navigators, I kind of felt the calling to go into ministry.

I was using that as an excuse to try to get out. The chaplain prayed for me and said, "Search out and seek what God wants you to do—not necessarily what you want to do, but what God wants you to do." I learned a valuable lesson at that time: to be content with my circumstances, as the apostle Paul encourages in the New Testament.

I've also learned that it's an ongoing lesson to be content. If we are content in our lives right now, it doesn't mean we are going to be content a year from now. We always have to search out and maintain that revolving door. After I learned contentment, I was able to come home on leave after eighteen months of being in Japan. Within a week of being back in Japan after my leave, I was told I needed to pick orders for my next duty station. Within six months, I was going to be moving again. God definitely blessed me and rewarded my contentment in that He allowed me to move to San Diego. Not only was I back stateside, but San Diego was only two hours away from my grandma, whom I rarely saw growing up. On top of that, my little brother was joining the Navy, and we got it arranged where I would be serving on the same ship with my brother for my last year in the Navy, which was his first year. It was like God was saying, "Thank you for being content in the situation I have given you." Because of this, I was also able to work with the Navigators for that year, and I attended Bible studies with them three days a week. I was either in church or in a Bible study. My faith really grew.

After serving four years, I came back home to Des Moines and went back to the church camp where I had grown up and worked. I got to know a guy named Clint, and when Clint's roommate moved out and got married, I moved in with him. During this time, I met my future wife. She was attending the same church I went to.

When I got cancer at age twenty-six, it drained my faith a lot. Jessie was seven months' pregnant with our first child. I was at work when my shoulder started hurting. I took Advil and Tylenol like crazy to try and kill the pain. I went to the doctor. He took an X-ray and sent me to a specialist. The specialist told me I just needed to strengthen my arm and wanted me to go to physical therapy, but before I had the chance I was lying in bed and felt a lump in the upper left chest area, under my arm. I went to the doctor, and he suspected a fatty tissue tumor, but he wanted me to see the surgeon. The surgeon was concerned after a CT scan and took out the tumor within a few days.

A week or two later the news came back that it was cancerous. They had it sent to Mayo, and the doctor called and told me over the phone. He said we had to be very aggressive with it, and he wanted to do radiation and chemo after they took out a wider margin. They took a couple of my ribs, eight inches each, and some muscle and tissue. They went right down to my lung and took some samples. The results came back clean, so they were confident they got all the cancer. The surgery was really hard on me. While I was at the hospital, I stopped breathing because I had too much morphine in my system. After the surgery, I woke up in intensive care on the ventilator and spent three days on that. I haven't told very many people, but I did see something very bright. I passed it off as being in an elevator or something, but it was tunnel-like with a lot of bright lights. This was when I stopped breathing and the hospital staff brought me back.

I was off work for thirteen months while I recovered from that surgery. I didn't receive any radiation or chemo, so I was fortunate there, but in the meantime my oldest was born in October. Jessie was having complications because of all the stress, so she was in and out of the hospital during the time I was still in the hospital. The day I was released from the hospital, I had to ride over to another hospital with my grandma because Jessie was fighting early labor. A couple of weeks later, Becky was born. That was a very trying time for me, but the biggest blessings out of that were Becky and that I was able to spend the first year of her life at home with her. As a dad, that very rarely happens, so I was very fortunate in that.

Fast-forward to today. I've got two children and have been cancer-free for twelve years. God has taught me so much through my trials. I've learned to depend on Him for all my needs. If He had decided twelve years ago to take me by His side, I would have been grateful. I'm also grateful He gave me another chance. I just pray I can live up to my potential in Him.

Steve and Rickey

Steve – I've had a lot of ups and downs in my life. Now, for the first time at sixty-six, I really feel complete and at peace, like I am united with God. I have no regrets, only positive things to look back on. I am very content with my life and am ready if He calls me home. I love my God, my church, and my family. It took me awhile to get to this point, and my story of the past shows this.

I grew up in the church. Different things in my life challenged me, and I got away from the church and God. It started when I graduated from high school; I got drafted in the army. I didn't have time to think about church, but while in basic training I went a few times. They would ask if we wanted to go to church. It didn't take me long to realize that, if we went to church, we didn't have to rake sand and move rocks.

Then I went to Vietnam, and that put me at my low point. I flew helicopters. I took the soldiers in and dropped them off. I spent two years over there, and I lost some friends; some were acquaintances, but some were good friends. I didn't want anything to do with the church or with God at that point.

There was a guy who had just come into the unit, and he slept on a bunk above me. One day he was supposed to be on my helicopter. He was a gunner but went on a different helicopter. The aircraft he was on hit a revetment, something that protects the helicopter from being hit, and it blew up. It went up in a ball of fire. We were right behind him, and I saw it. Our pilot was going to move because there was ammunition going off everywhere, but I jumped out of our helicopter and ran over to him. I held him in my arms until an ambulance got there. He later died in Japan. That was a real low point.

Sometimes you hear about people beginning to use heavy substances while in the military. I never smoked a cigarette until I went to Vietnam. I didn't get into drugs, but I did begin to drink heavily. I was probably born an alcoholic; my dad's side of the family loved their beer. In Vietnam, there were two types of people. There were people on the ground working on maintenance and trucks. They did the drugs, a lot of hard drugs. Then there were people in the flight platoon. We drank. If anybody in the flight platoon was caught smoking, they were out; it was an unwritten rule. The beer was shipped by boat, and the drugs came from Burma, Thailand, and Cambodia.

At one point, our unit was next to the South China Sea, and it was a very dangerous sea. A guy who had not even been there a month went out to the sea and started swimming, trying to swim home. The sharks got him. Whether he was on drugs at the time or not in the right frame of mind, nobody knows. He died in the middle of the night.

I came back and got married, but church was not a part of me. We went to Germany for three and a half years and never once went to church. Everything I did was for the army, which resulted in me letting go of my family.

We came back from Germany, and I had an opportunity to go to school and learn about the Black Hawk helicopter, which is the main helicopter that is used today. That became my life. I was "Mr. Black Hawk." If there were problems, I could tell the engineers how to rectify them. They would often call me, and we would brainstorm together.

I got away from Christ and my family, and at that point they were on their own. I had let go. I had a title, and I wanted to keep that title. I put that helicopter above everybody and taught thousands of people. You might remember the story of *Black Hawk Down* and the one man who survived. I trained him. I also trained two of the crew chiefs that were killed. I went all over the United States teaching these people, showing them how it worked. Like I said, I let my kids go.

After two failed marriages and retirement from the army, I bought a house and moved to the southern part of Des Moines. That was really a bad time in my life, probably my lowest point. I asked a woman to move in with me. She had a daughter who was supposed to leave after staying for a while. I got home one night, and her ex-husband was standing in the kitchen. We got into an argument, and the next thing I knew her daughter had me up against the corner wall and a cop was there. They said I was verbally abusing them and putting their lives in jeopardy. They said they didn't know if I was going to attack them or what. Well, how can you attack someone when you are stuck against the wall? I went to jail. I had money in the bank for bail, but my mother would not take the money out because my sisters told her to "just leave him there to rot." I had never done anything to my sisters.

In jail, you have a card for money, and a guy loaned me some so I could make a call to get a bondsman. I got out of there and received a deferred judgment. You wouldn't believe how many people suddenly become religious in jail.

The judge told me that since it was three against one, she had no choice but to defer me. I was away for ten days, and when I got back I found that they had stripped the house. I had an itemized list, but the judge said it was irrelevant to the case. I never got anything back, including the thousands of dollars the woman I lived with had accumulated on my credit card.

Then I met Rickey.

Rickey – Since my daughter's recent death, I don't try to understand why things happen. A testimony always seems to be filled with good things, but it doesn't always have to be. God has helped me get through this. I just started going to church in the last few years. I've always believed, and I've always prayed, but I didn't go to church very often, just periodically. My grandmother was my inspiration. She talked about God, and I learned the Lord's Prayer from her. I sometimes say to God, "What are You doing?" This has been the closest I've felt to Him. My grandson got me involved in church. He used to ride his bike five miles to church, and I always asked him if I could give him a ride. He was the one who latched on, and I started to go with him.

Steve and I met online. My husband died the year before. We had been married forty-seven years; he had cancer for thirteen of them. After he died, I got a dog, and I thought, *Well, the dog doesn't talk to me. It doesn't take me to dinner.* So I got online and had maybe three dates with three different gentlemen, but it was a lot of work. I hadn't dated for over fifty years. My rule was, if they didn't have a picture and they smoked, I wasn't talking to them. Steve's profile had no picture, and he smoked ("Trying to quit," it said). But he said on his page, "I don't expect much from anyone, and I hope no one would expect much from me." I had to respond. I said, "That is no way to get anywhere. That's not a good line. You need to change that!" Then we started talking. We were supposed to meet at Olive Garden, but it was packed, so we went to Panera Bread and had lunch. I came down to Des Moines for a year. A year and a month later we got married. We've been married for three years.

Steve – At that point, some higher power was doing this. Like I said, I was at the lowest point in my life when I went through this jail deal. Vietnam was really bad, really low, because I lost people, but I think this was the lowest because I lost everything. When I met Rickey, she was going to church with Thadius, her grandson. One Saturday, out of the blue, Rickey said she was going to church, and I asked if I could go along. Things started to come together to where we are today. I feel the closest to God now.

Rickey – So I guess we do have a story. I should be thankful. I have had like five experiences where I shouldn't be here. I had blood poisoning from a hangnail, and then I had a blood clot that went through my heart and lung. I shouldn't be here, but there is a reason I am here. When you start thinking about the bad stuff, you forget to think about the good stuff. I am thankful for what I have and try not to dwell on the bad stuff.

Darrel and Brenda

Brenda – This is my Father's world. Everything we see in nature shows God. He is all around us. When I get up in the morning, I see the sun and I think of Him. I see the moon at night as I go for walks. It's quiet and peaceful, and I can see the stillness of God's voice speaking loudly to everyone through the animals, insects, and wind. I can see God in the handiwork of the green grass; each leaf is different on a tree, just like each flower and snowflake. Who else could have designed all that?

Nature is a huge part of my life and where I really see Him. Psalm 19 says, "The heavens declare the glory of God; the skies proclaim the work of his hands. Day after day they pour forth speech; night after night they reveal knowledge. They have no speech, they use no words; no sound is heard from them. Yet their voice goes out into all the earth, their words to the ends of the world."

Darrel – I went into the service in December 1965 at the age of nineteen. I was on the Pacific for three weeks before reaching Vietnam. My role was being supply sergeant for an infantry company. Unfortunately, I was the one who had to inventory personal items when we had a KIA (Killed in Action). Their duffel bags were in a supply room, so I had to open the bags and sort out the military and personal items. The first four or five bags I sorted through really bothered me because I trained with all these guys. I saw pictures of wives, girlfriends, and parents. Everybody had a story. After a while, I just had to block it out; not that I was coldhearted, but I had to block it out so it wouldn't get to me. It's unfortunate.

A buddy of mine from high school was in the service with me the whole time. I had somebody I could relate to. Our common ground was church. The good Lord was watching over him because he never got a scratch on him, even though he was in infantry. I knew God was there when we were in Vietnam, but I was young and invincible. I used to say, "I can do anything." I put my trust in Him, but I didn't pray every day for Him to protect me. I just knew, in my mind, that He did. I didn't worry if I was going to make it or not. I just did the job and whatever happened, happened.

As I get older, I rely more on God and His direction than when I was young. Faith is a maturity thing. We start out almost like little babies in the faith and then continue to grow throughout our lives as long as we work at it and want it. I grew up in a church, and I made a profession of faith. I learned the Catechism, and it was all good. Now I feel like, as a couple, we are learning more. It's more of a personal faith. I think some people are afraid of being Christians because they think they have to be perfect. You can learn as you go, and it's different for everybody. You don't conform to the things of the world; you watch your language and try to be a positive influence, letting your light shine.

"Do not conform to the pattern of this world, but be transformed by the renewing of your mind. Then you will be able to test and approve what God's will is—his good, pleasing and perfect will" (Romans 12:2).

CHAPTER 3

Missing

The loss of a loved one damages the soul, but because of trusting in God and Jesus Christ, these individuals know that being reunited is possible.

"My flesh and my heart may fail, but God is the strength of my heart and my portion forever."

Psalm 73:26

Carrie

We were raised in a Christian home and had a fabulous upbringing. All five of us kids were treated equally. When I got older, I started running with the wrong crowd of people, and I knew it wasn't right. I felt pressure from some of my sisters because they were straight-A students and I wasn't. Since I was a good athlete, I ran around with the athletes. We would drink, party, and have sex. I knew my life was going downhill. I never did drugs; I just drank a lot of alcohol. I got pregnant when I was a senior in high school. I didn't tell my mom and dad right away. When I did tell them, my mom wanted me to have an abortion. I told them I was not going to do that. Mom knew that wasn't the right thing to do, but we were living in a small community, and she just wanted it to go away.

My sisters were in college at nursing school, and I could've easily just gone there, but I decided to put my baby up for adoption. I knew somebody would love her. My mom and dad wanted to keep her because she was their first grandchild, but I said no because they had raised all of us kids. It just wasn't fair to raise grandchildren too. She was born two days before my first niece was born. I was in the hospital having Heather when Judy, my sister-in-law, was in the hospital having Nicky. That was really hard.

It was tough getting back into the community. My parents said I couldn't go to my graduation because I was nine months' pregnant. Later I found out it was really the school administration that said I couldn't go. My parents went to my graduation, and I stayed home. They had a graduation party for me afterwards. Can you imagine what I put my parents through and how strong they were to do that? I don't ever remember asking the Lord to help me get through it. But now, as I've gotten older, I know my parents and family members were all praying for me. And He did.

Randy and I got married, and after fourteen years of infertility and surgery, I found out I couldn't have any kids. That was really tough, especially seeing all my sisters and brother having kids and knowing I couldn't have them. I thought God was punishing me for giving up Heather. I thought He was saying, *I gave you a child, but you rejected her and gave her away.* As I've gotten older (I'm now fifty-seven), I realize that wasn't true at all. After fourteen years, we decided to adopt. We knew we were going to do everything humanly possible to make it happen, but we left it up to the Lord if it was meant to be. Then we were blessed with a little boy. He was a month old when we got him. We chose not to tell any of our folks that we were planning to adopt.

Before we got him, we had three days to get a nursery set up. We called Randy's parents and made up an excuse to get together. We said, "Sorry we missed your birthday. We'd like to meet you in Humbolt to give you a cake." I told them we were going to have my parents meet up too. That wasn't a big deal. They knew each other because they lived fairly close. When I walked in, I was carrying a camcorder. They said, "Oh, did you get a new camcorder?" I said, "Yes, I got a new camcorder. I'm just playing with it to see what it does." Then Randy came walking in with a baby. Nobody could believe it! Everybody was crying. We didn't tell anybody because fourteen years of infertility was tough physically. I could go through a lot with my body, but I couldn't handle the mental stress and everybody asking if we'd heard anything yet. We took him all over and introduced him to people. That was such a blessing.

I still felt a void in my life, though. I told myself I should be happy because I had a son, but I couldn't have my own child. I needed to try and find my daughter. Because of all the prayers, searching, and phone calls, I found her within a year. She was in college. I knew if I didn't contact her, she would be gone because she would be somewhere else after college. I wrote her a letter and sent her a picture of us so she could see who was writing the letter. I gave her my phone number. She called me, and we talked for about two hours. We laughed and laughed. It was such a special time to have her in my life. People who have never been through that don't understand how you long for your child. There's a piece of you missing, and, until you can get that piece back into the puzzle, you just don't feel complete. She completed me.

Terry and Mary

Mary – As I have gotten older, I know my faith has grown. I can look back and see the events of my life unfold in ways I would not have thought imaginable or in ways I would not have chosen. But I know that God is a Sovereign God and that His ways and His timing are perfect. As His child, I knew He was going to mold me into the one He wanted me to be. Some of this molding I resisted and some I didn't. Yet other times I had no choice. The good events and the harsh trials drew me to become more dependent on Him. As I look back on my life, I am grateful for His design of my life, and I know He isn't done with me yet. He is still designing me!

I lost my first husband at age thirty-three. We had a three-year-old girl and a five-month-old baby boy. Wow, what a trial! But because of my faith and knowing that His promises in the Scriptures were for me, I knew God had a plan for us, and He wasn't going to forget about us. During this time I intimately experienced Him as my provider, comforter, strength, rock, shoulder to cry on, guardian, and Father to my children. However, the greatest was knowing that He is my heavenly Father who, I believe, cried right along with me.

The awesomeness of His plan for my life unfolded when He led me to my second husband, Terry. Terry and I both attended the same church, and he was going through his own trial at that time. I had admired Terry as a husband to his wife and father to his daughter, never thinking that he would be my husband one day. Oh, but here is where His perfect plan plays out. Sadly, Terry's wife divorced him. Terry and I were married a couple years later. He adopted my two children and raised them as his own. Not only did I gain another daughter from his first marriage, but we then had a son together who is now twenty-two years old. Our God is an awesome God.

Terry – God's presence in my life was reinforced while doing my job as a police detective in the city where I worked and then when I became involved in a bank robbery investigation. Three men and one female were committing the bank robbery. A witness saw them going into the bank and coming out quickly, so she called the police. I heard the radio call, along with several other officers in the area. The witness described the vehicle that the suspects left in. I responded to the area and met up with two patrol cars that were behind the suspect's vehicle. The suspects were not stopping. They entered onto the interstate, but they pulled over because their vehicle was damaged. When they pulled over, the driver jumped out of the vehicle and came charging toward the officers with a gun. Another suspect was lying down prone across the front seat of the suspect's vehicle and pointed a gun at the first officer. That suspect was shot and killed. The other one was running toward the second officer. I had just gotten out of my car. The suspect was between the officer and me. The officer confronted the suspect, who had a gun in his hand. The officer killed the suspect, firing numerous times; however, only some of the rounds hit the suspect.

Although I was directly in the line of fire, none of the other rounds hit me or my vehicle. I knew it was a God-thing, as the officer fired right in my direction. I later had to testify at the grand jury investigation, which gave me an opportunity to share about this being a God-thing. The county attorney didn't understand how I didn't get shot. I explained that God was present and protected me.

We later found out the suspects' guns were BB guns. We couldn't tell the difference between real guns and the BB guns during the confrontation. They looked identical to the real guns they were modeled after. We also found out the suspects' vehicle was damaged after striking a curb during the initial escape from the bank, which explained why he stopped on the interstate. It is our belief that the suspects were going to confront the officers and try to get their guns. Information received during the investigation also indicated that the suspects vowed not to go back to prison.

All the officers involved, except me, took a medical retirement after that situation. God protected me. I had faith that He was the reason I survived and that He would carry me through this trial in my life. Was it sad watching somebody die in front of me? Yes, it was. It wouldn't have made a difference whether he was the suspect or not. The officers did everything right. When suspects come after you with guns, you have to do what you have to do.

I also praise God for bringing me from the despair of divorce and blessing me with a beautiful, loving wife, more children, and now grandchildren. I have seen God's presence many times over the years and thank Him continually for Mary and my family. We have seen His blessings in the lives of our children. They each have stories to tell about God orchestrating their lives and carrying them through difficult situations. He has given all four of them godly spouses for which we are eternally grateful. Once again, our God is an awesome God, worthy to be praised!

Heath and Wendy

Wendy – A time where I felt God was near was when we lost our first baby. That was probably my first real painful thing in life. Unfortunately, those are the times we draw close to God. At first I felt very alone because it had never happened in my family. Our church family became closer to us during that time. People were amazing; they would come up to me and tell me they had been in that situation. They knew how I was feeling, and they showed me such compassion and love. There's peace knowing God is good. I look around at what we have now, and we are so blessed.

We had an amazing doctor, but she kept saying to take morphine because

of the painful contractions. She knew the baby was gone, so she didn't want me to endure any more pain than I already had. I was completely out of it when I delivered him. I can't take any of that back or change it, and I've accepted it, but I struggled for a long time. They asked us if we wanted to bury him or if they could send him off to do testing. We were kids then and didn't really know what we were doing. We had to make quick decisions that we now regret. We didn't bury him, so I have tried to live with that. For a while, I could really feel God giving me peace about it, and now He is getting me through it and giving me peace with my decisions.

When I met Heath, he was kind of my lifesaver. We know that God has a plan for everyone, and He definitely sent Heath into my life to lead me to Christ. I met him when I was eighteen. He grew up in a Christian home. I had never read the Bible. My mom taught me the Lord's Prayer and a few things, but it meant nothing to me. He started to invite me to his church. We got married when I was twenty-three, and I made a profession of faith right before that. I called myself a Christian at that time, but I didn't know what I know today. People are constantly growing, and I was too. At twenty-three, I wanted to start to know about God, but I was still not living my life the way I wanted to. It really is a prize when you can look back and see where your life changed because of your relationship with Christ. I wanted to be more like Him.

Heath – Our youngest daughter prays for people all the time. When someone at our church had breast cancer, Lacy prayed every day. When our dentist had a tumor, our daughter prayed. She is only six years old. Both of them are better now, but it might not have gone that way. She knew the importance of prayer and that it was real.

Luke – I pray that when I fight with my sisters God will forgive me.

Wendy – God healed Luke's legs when he was eleven months old. He woke up one morning, and his legs would not work. We found out he had a virus in his spinal cord causing inflammation in his legs. He was

paralyzed and spent a week in intensive care. Slowly, the feeling in his legs came back. We found out there was not a very good chance of him walking, but he started walking by the time he was eighteen months old. By the time we left the hospital, he had taken three little crawls. They thought that was a good sign. When we went back to his appointment, I asked the neurologist, "How lucky are we?" He said, "Well, I don't usually tell people this, but you are very lucky; 90 percent would be wheelchair-bound." For a long time, I called him my miracle baby because God totally healed him. We had major prayer warriors out there.

Heath – Right now, I feel very close to God. I'm doing an online bachelor's degree program through Liberty University, working toward a bachelor's degree in religion. Every eight weeks, I take a new course that is worth three credits. I've been studying church history and theology. The next one I'm taking is on the book of Acts. I've taken courses on the Old and New Testaments. That is what I do every night after the kids go to bed. I feel like I'm already using what I have learned by teaching Sunday school and at work. I will retire from the army soon, so this will be something to fall back on. It's not really my goal to get a job with this degree; I just want to be a better Christian and grow in my faith.

Wendy – It is a blessing for me because I still have all these questions since I didn't grow up attending church. He is so knowledgeable. Often, during the day, I will text him at work to ask him a biblical question, or I will say to the kids, "Dad will know the answer." It's like I have my own little pastor I can just talk to. He gives me my strength when I need it. If I need encouragement, he is always there to encourage me.

Heath – In high school, I never read a book. Now I have to read several books—big ones. I know that is one thing God has helped me with. He has helped me learn how to read faster and has made me want to read because that was never part of my life before. He really started to change my life with this new desire for school. The real challenge is stopping

and going to bed. Some days, it is my favorite part of the day: reading, studying, writing, and then applying it.

Bob and Sharon

Bob – I told my son, "God has a sense of humor." He said, "Really?" I said, "Well, He made me!" Most people know I have a "different" sense of humor.

I often think about where God plants us. We were both raised in northwest Iowa, and I taught school and lived in Sioux County for ten years. I look back to that time, and that's where we all gave our lives to the Lord, all four of us. Even though Boyden was a good place to live, we became concerned about staying there because I had left teaching and saw no future there.

I saw an advertisement in the newspaper for a salesman for a music store. I called the store owner, who then flew me to Des Moines to interview for the job. The music store owner didn't offer me the job because I said I wouldn't work on Sunday. I then called my old band director, who gave me the name of another music store that needed a salesman and a carpenter. I interviewed with the second music store owner, was hired, and began working in Des Moines. Everything flowed together. We sold our house in Boyden, bought a house in Des Moines, Sharon was offered an accounting job, and we moved. This all happened in six weeks. We saw God's hand in the timing.

I think the Lord really spoke to me when our daughter, Patti, was diagnosed with colon cancer. She lived two years after the diagnosis. It is difficult to watch a loved one live with and then die of cancer. Patti spent her last few months preparing her children for her death. She would talk with each child every evening before they went to bed about what kind of day they had and prayed with each one. It helps to know that we will be together again in heaven.

Our son, Tim, has been struggling with health issues recently and was in critical condition at one point. It was difficult to think we might lose our second child due to illness, but he was released from the hospital and is getting better. I have also had some health issues recently and wondered what the Lord was trying to tell me.

I rely on Romans 8:28, "And we know that in all things, God works for the good of those who love him, who have been called according to his purpose."

Sharon – I was the second of five children. My mother and father were both from large families and raised in northwest Iowa. Bob and I lived in small towns within twenty miles of each other. We met when he was invited by my pastor to direct our church choir. Bob was attending Buena Vista College, studying vocal and instrumental music.

We came to know the Lord after we were married and had our two children. Even though we struggled financially, God was good to us. Bob quit teaching and went to work for a local construction company. Every month, we went deeper into debt. We moved to Des Moines and have lived here for almost forty years.

My walk with God has made me realize that life without Him is nothing. He has been so good to us, even in the difficulties we've had. I do know that our life struggles are no different from those of other people. Sometimes the walk is difficult, but I believe what I've read and studied—we, as believers, will spend eternity in heaven at the feet of God's throne.

Caitlyn

While growing up, my dad never went to church. My mom went some, but neither one talked much about it. They wanted me to go, though. When my dad passed away, I still went, but I didn't go as often. I didn't feel like I wanted to be there. I just went because my friends were there.

At one point I was going to a church, and the leader asked someone to read John 3:16. To me that seemed so strange because I thought most people had that memorized. It made me realize that the church I was attending was not the right place for me. I changed churches and went back to where I went as a child. I found that I was not hanging out with the same people anymore. I started hanging out with people from my new church. I became friends with a great girl, and I saw how God was really working through her. She was an inspiration, and seeing this encouraged me to dive into everything more.

As a teenager, it's hard to do the right thing, but I definitely saw myself changing. I knew where God wanted me to be. In February 2014, when I was fifteen, I went to a conference called TEC (Teens Encounter Christ). It was an eye-opening experience where you walk through the Stations of the Cross—everything that Jesus went through to get to where we are today. I thought, *How could You sacrifice Your son for everyone else on earth?* That really got to me. After that weekend, I was on this crazy "God high." Around this time, I was swearing a lot. I was around those who did it, and whenever I swore I knew immediately it was wrong. Knowledge that you are sinning is huge. It's really helped me in my faith.

Since then, it's been hard to stay on the right track and have a "God high," but I have stayed close to my friends who are Christians, and that keeps me on track. I let them know what I am going through and what I'm feeling. For a couple of months, I felt like God had abandoned me. A lot had been going on at home (fighting between my mom and stepdad) that added a lot of stress, so I felt distant from God again.

Recently, I went to TEC again, and I was leading the students. Seeing them come to faith and seeing God's love in action really put me back on that track this past week. I know everything is in God's hands, and I can't control anything. I think, even as an adult, it's hard to put your full trust in God, to be still, and to focus on reading God's Word, especially when there are so many distractions.

My dad died on December 7, 2008, when I was ten. He was not sick for very long. It was a disease called hantavirus, caused by rodents' urine and feces. We don't know where he got it. There were floods that year, and he was working a lot of overtime for the railroads in Cedar Rapids. He also worked on bridges that had collapsed in the area. The virus stays in the system for a couple of months. He was stubborn and didn't go to the doctor. He didn't tell anyone he wasn't feeling well until the week he died.

He was getting flu-like symptoms and started puking and coughing. The morning before his death, we went to church because my parents were going to be godparents to the baby of some friends. My dad had these symptoms, but he was determined not to miss it. After the ceremony, he still was not feeling well, so we took him home. My grandpa had been in the hospital during the week, and he was going to be released that day. My mom was going to the hospital to pick him up. As my grandpa was getting released, my dad called and said, "I need you to come get me now. I need to get to the hospital. I'm feeling really dizzy."

My brother and I had gone out with our friends. As my mom and grandpa walked in the door, my dad was getting ready to pass out. My mom caught him. Grandpa called 911, and an ambulance came. By the time we got to the house after all this, he was on a gurney. I remember saying to him, "I love you, Daddy." Then they took him to the hospital.

As a kid, I knew he was sick, but I thought he was going to be okay. I don't know if it was God calming my nerves, but I just didn't feel like it was all that bad. Then my mom called and said, "You need to come to the hospital." Her best friend picked us up and took us to the hospital. Everyone in our family was there, including some of the church family. I didn't think it was very bad, so I wondered why everyone was there. Eventually, my mom pulled us into a smaller room where my grandparents were, and she said, "I don't think your dad is going to make it." My brother and I both started crying. He was seven at the time. I remember, as I came out of the room, all my family was around, but I went to Chris and Judy, two members of my church family. I just felt like that was where I needed to be. They were my comfort. I remember coloring and talking to them about my dad. I drew pictures of what we talked about. God was working that night, comforting me with the people who were there. My dad died that night around midnight.

I cried that night and at the funeral, but I didn't shed one tear at the visitation. I knew I needed to be strong. I felt like I was helping my mom out by being that way. I felt like I received that strength from God because I was only ten and knew everything that was going on. What ten-year-old would not be crying after losing her dad?

When I look back and see all these things God has done in my life, all I can say is, "Wow!" In one week, I felt all of that. Yet at times I still turn away from God, which is so disappointing. I know my dad wants me to be with the Lord, and that helps to keep me focused. I am so much happier because I know I don't have to carry my burdens on my shoulders. Everything is in God's hands.

CHAPTER 4

Heaviness

Personal problems can weaken us. Depression can take its toll and hope can be lost. God promises that He will always be with us, and He will deliver us out of darkness.

"Do not fear, for I have redeemed you; I have called you by name, you are mine. When you pass through the waters, I will be with you; and through the rivers, they shall not overwhelm you; when you walk through fire you shall not be burned, and the flame shall not consume you. For I am the Lord your God, the Holy One of Israel, your Savior."
Isaiah 43:1-3

Betty

I was raised in a Christian home, and for several years I thought that if I was good enough, I would be a Christian too. Before I was two years old, I was diagnosed with a bone disease, so I was in a brace for many months and had to learn to walk all over again. Later, as I was still battling some of the effects of the disease, a well-meaning gal from our church told me the disease and pain were because of my personal sins. Since I had been diagnosed at such an early age, I could not imagine what I had done that was so awful God hated me or wanted to punish me so much.

For many years, I didn't really feel loved by God. I sang the song

"Jesus Loves Me" in Sunday school and Bible school, but I wasn't really sure it was true for me. People would say, "Even if you were the only one alive, Jesus still would have come to earth and died for your sin." I always thought that was meant for everyone but me. I also had a family member who was always putting me down and was rather verbally abusive, so I felt unlovable in many ways. I grew up with no sense of self-worth and was extremely shy.

Then one day, when my children were very little, I realized I needed to make a personal commitment to Jesus Christ. I accepted Him as my Lord and Savior, committed my life to Him, and received the infilling of the Holy Spirit. I attended church regularly by sneaking in the back pew and then slipping out as soon as the service was over. I finally reached the point where I was comfortable teaching Sunday school or Bible school in the preschool level, but I said that I would never lead an adult class. However, I began praying that God would use me for His glory. He said, "How can I use you when you won't look at or talk to anyone?"

Suddenly, after starting to pray about this, I woke up around two or three in the morning with a dream or vision of me sitting in front of a large group of people with a puppet on my lap while talking and singing about the Lord. I argued, "I can't do that! I can't even talk to or look at one person, much less a whole group!" The next night it happened again, and I argued, "I don't know anything about ventriloquism, and I don't know where to learn." The third night when it happened, I argued, "I don't have the money for the resources, and I don't know where to get them even if I did." By the fourth night, I was too tired to argue anymore, and it finally dawned on me that God was trying to tell me something. So that night I said, "Okay, God, if this is what You want me to do, You are going to have to show me how."

God began waking me up in the middle of the night with script and song ideas, so I would get up and write them down. I tried to figure out how to make a puppet with limited resources and no pattern. Then I found myself with written scripts, music, and a puppet, but I didn't know what to do with them. The next thing I knew, I was asked to present a ministry of music at my church. I knew I couldn't get up in front of everyone without something to focus on, so I decided to use the puppet and one of the scripts I had written down. I thought I would be thrown out of the church on my ear for using a puppet, but I did it. Not only was I not thrown out of church, but someone was visiting from another church and asked me to come do a program at their family retreat. During the retreat, someone else asked me to present daily programs at their church's Bible school. It just snowballed from there. I got over my shyness by going around meeting new people wherever God called me to go. I found that as long as I had a puppet on my hand, using an illusion trick, or wearing a clown nose and makeup, I could stand in front of people and tell them about Christ.

Now I have trunks full of props and puppets. I got a puppet in Belize on a mission trip and another one in Kentucky when our church went there to host a Bible school. One of my favorites is a lion that was sent to me when I shattered my ankle. I know this sounds really crazy, but here was a grown woman lying in a hospital bed and getting so excited over a puppet. Later on, I received a matching one. I do character-building puppet programs for our church's preschool using lots of different characters and animals, so now I have a brother and sister lion team.

God used the puppet ministry to help me overcome my shyness, and in 1983 He used a spiritual renewal weekend called Cursillo to start breaking down the walls of my insecurity. He showed me that He could love me through my brothers and sisters in Christ, and He revealed to me that I no longer needed to hide behind props to be able to witness for Him.

One year, while I was working at a Cursillo weekend at Teen Challenge, I was praying that the guys there would know how much God loved them. I thought that if they knew He had died just for them, it would really change their lives. Suddenly I had a vision of Jesus sitting right in front of me. He smiled and said, "Yes, and I did it for you too!" That was a huge, life-changing moment for me as I realized He loved and accepted me just as I was, but He loved me too much to let me stay that way!

God also led me to a wonderful in-depth Bible study called Bible

Study Fellowship International. Shortly after I started attending, I was asked to interview about becoming part of the leadership team. During the interview, the teaching leader remarked that with all my experience working with children I should become a children's leader. I suddenly heard a voice saying, "No, I think God is pushing me out of my comfort zone to become an adult discussion leader." Instantly, I wondered, *Who said that?* and realized it had been my voice, but the Holy Spirit's decision. Now, after twenty years of leading women in Bible study, I look back and laugh about how God made me eat my words about never leading adults!

As for who God is? He is everything I need! He is my Creator, Savior, Redeemer, Provider, Counselor, Great Physician . . . and the list goes on and on. I like to call Him my true and ultimate Best Friend Forever!

Michelle

I grew up in southeast Kansas surrounded by farmland and cattle drives. I was homeschooled, so my siblings and I ended up being really close. After school, we would go outside and play with each other, using our imaginations to disappear into the lands of Narnia and Star Trek. We would explore all that pastureland, so we grew up kind of wild.

We grew up Reformed Baptist. When I decided to go to college for art, my parents and siblings were very supportive, but some of my extended family members were not. I had such a drive to go into art, but my family thought I would not make enough money. One of my aunts thinks that I am going to be poor my whole life. There is a high demand for artists; you just have to be willing to put your best effort in it. I'm not doing it for the money. I'm doing it because I love it.

I think it's funny how, as humans, we focus on the bad and not the good. God can use really hard things in people's lives to draw them closer to Him and change them. Even though life can be hard, hard things can actually be a very good thing. Until I was about eighteen, everything was really great with my family and my dad. We always knew he had a temper, but because he was working for another company, it was never really directed at the family. In 2007, we moved from South Texas to Kansas, and Dad started his own business as a drywaller. Since we were homeschooled, the boys would go with him to work after school. My sister and I didn't think anything of it. We just stayed around home. Then, two years later, my brother wanted to join the military. I was about twenty-one at the time, and my sister was seventeen.

My dad insisted that my sister and I start working with him since my brother, Josh, would be gone. My sister and I were super skinny, and we could only lift so much. The first day working with Dad was a terrible shock. My sister and I came home that day, went to our mom, and asked, "Mom, do you realize Dad is being kind of abusive at work?" He had been yelling and screaming at the boys and throwing things at them. While holding up drywall, Dad would kick them in the stomach. It was really scary. The boys had not told anyone about the abuse, so we had no idea. My mom had no idea. My sister and I, because we were girls, were a little bit more emotional. It was such a shock. So the situation came out, and the pastor of our church started working with my dad one-on-one on Wednesday nights for about a year. But Dad wouldn't give him the whole story and would say, "Yes, it is getting better," when it was really getting worse. If anything, Dad was just getting angrier because he had to deal with it. It got to the point where the pastor took us out of there. My mom and youngest brother left home for a month but eventually went back. But Josh, Sarah, and I didn't go back.

We grew up in a lifestyle that taught girls not to go to college or work at a job. My brother had only ever worked for my dad, so we didn't know how to pay bills or get jobs. I had been babysitting some during that time, but we didn't know how to do a lot of things. We found ourselves in this huge world all on our own. It came to the point where my brother, sister, and I literally had nothing but God. It was scary, but the church rallied around us. The church is so small—only about twenty people. They brought us a bunch of things they didn't need anymore. We ended up with a mattress, pots and pans, and a coffeemaker.

In the summer of 2011, we spent three months in a room in the back of that church. We finally found a little house, and my brother found a job with the pastor's help. Things were still pretty bad with our dad, who had stopped going to church. We siblings were still close, but there was a lot to work through. We tried to help Dad but hoped the distance would make him realize everything he had been doing. We probably could have called the police, and I would have if it had gotten to that point, but we tried to give him a chance. We love him. We weren't bitter, but we knew we couldn't let him keep doing this.

We spent a year on our own in that house. We all had our own jobs. It wasn't like we made a lot of money, but we were so happy. We knew God was taking care of us, and we could see Him in everything. He was sustaining us and caring for us. Some nights we came home exhausted from our jobs, but we were so happy just to be together. We would turn up the music and do these silly crazy fun dances. (We could get away with it too, since we lived in the country and didn't have neighbors.) We would spend hours talking to each other. It was amazing, even though it was so hard. We were aware of how much God loved us because this could have gone so bad, but God provided for all of us.

God used that situation to show us that all we have in life is Him. When you are going through trials, you feel His love so much more than you do when things are good. Sometimes life is so hard, and I end up crying in the shower praying, *God, this is hard! I don't like this. I don't understand why, but I know You love me.* I know that Romans 8:28 is true. No matter what, God is going to catch me, even though I feel like I am free-falling and have no idea where I am going.

Recently, things with my dad have gotten better. We think God saved him. Last May, I went home for a week to visit my family, and Dad seemed like himself again—the dad we were used to and who wasn't abusive and angry. Things slowly got better. During that trip, my dad and I talked from eleven at night until three the next morning. It was a new, different dad—even better than the dad he had been. I felt like I could trust him again not to be emotionally abusive or judgmental. I was able to open up, and he cared by being sensitive and gentle. It was completely different from everything he used to be. I can only look back now and think, *Wow, God is really working in him.* It's amazing to see how God can change someone's life and how, even though trials are really hard and sad, God uses all that pain to make us dependent on Him and to run to Him. I would never change that whole experience because God used it to build us up, mold us, and help us grow in so many ways.

My ultimate goal is to glorify God with my artwork and to write children's books. I really admire C.S. Lewis and Tolkien. I admire Lewis especially because he was such a devout Christian, and he used his gifts to glorify God—even in children's stories! Ever since I was about fourteen, I wanted to do the same thing that Tolkien and Lewis did with their work. I have been writing since then and started illustrating because I didn't want someone else to come in and illustrate my stuff. I know exactly the way it looks in my mind. That's why I illustrate. I hope people might read my stories one day and find comfort in them.

Patty

I grew up in a Lutheran home where we went to church every Sunday. God has always meant a lot to me. When I was young, I tried to be good and do everything right. I would tell my sisters to do what was right or correct people when they were doing something wrong. As I got older, I told myself there were things I would never do, like smoke, drink, and have sex before marriage. But when I began training to be a nurse at Iowa Methodist Hospital, I started running around with kids who were much different from what I'd been used to in high school. I went home with them on weekends and smoked, drank alcohol, and did other things I never dreamed I would do. What the Lord showed me was that I was not good, and I didn't do everything right. I was very self-righteous, proud, and arrogant to think I was always good. I even went to the extreme in thinking that I didn't sin. The Lord used that time in my life to show me I was a sinner.

A Bible study started in the nurses' dorm, and so of course I went because I was a "Christian." An older woman named Amy was teaching straight from the Bible. I had no concept of what she meant as her lessons were all about a relationship with Jesus and being saved. That same phrase was expressed at a Billy Graham event I attended soon after high school graduation called Expo '72 in Dallas. I had heard about Jesus my entire life, but not about having a personal relationship with Him or being saved. In my mind, going to church was more about doing the right thing and being good. No one had ever explained what the Scriptures meant or told me about the entire redemption story like Amy did. "If we claim to be without sin, we deceive ourselves and the truth is not in us" (1 John 1:8). In John 14:6 Jesus says, "I am the way and the truth and the life. No one comes to the Father except through me." I combined those two verses and realized if you think you have no sin, Jesus is not in you! I repented of my sin and received Jesus as my personal Savior. My very own personal relationship with Him began early in 1973, and I was saved. Now I knew Jesus was In me!

My relationship with Jesus Christ has grown over the years, and He has been faithful to help me grow. My marriage was extremely difficult for a long time. Jerry and I both are very strong-willed and polar opposites in so many ways. It's a good thing we threw out the word "divorce" as an option before marriage! Our fights were loud, heated, and went long into the night. We determined to never go to sleep angry with one another and give the devil an opportunity to win. Sometimes it took until 3 a.m., but we would get things settled. God has worked miracles, and we are closer now than ever and celebrated our fortieth anniversary on August 9, 2015. To God be the glory!

Health problems have been tutors to shape me in Christlikeness as well. Twenty years ago, my neck began to turn involuntarily toward the right. I have a neurological disease that makes the muscles in my neck and shoulders contract in severe spasms. In desperation, I searched the Psalms for help and found relief. "It was good for me to be afflicted so that I might learn your decrees" (Psalm 119:71). Psalm 119:75-76 reads, "I know, Lord, that your laws are righteous, and that in faithfulness you have afflicted me. May your unfailing love be my comfort, according to your promise to your servant." The promises in God's Word have lifted and helped me through to this day. I have discovered that chronic pain results in a constant battle with self-centeredness. Pain wants to turn my focus inward, but whenever I'd have pity parties, no one would come! I have found that if I keep my focus upward toward the Lord, and outward toward others, the pain is much more manageable.

The next health trial was an aneurysm behind my left eye that initially caused extreme anxiety and stress. Nearly every day I would wonder if this was my last day to live. God's Word, once again, was my comfort and help. Philippians 4:6-7 says, "Do not be anxious about anything [I wrote in my Bible, "Not even aneurysms"], but in every situation, by prayer and petition, with thanksgiving, present your requests to God. And the peace of God, which transcends all understanding, will guard your hearts and your minds in Jesus Christ." Peace is what I needed more than anything, and that's what God taught me through having an aneurysm.

A true joy of being a mother is when your kids are grown, they marry, and have babies of their own. Our daughter Lydia was expecting our first grandchild, but our joy turned to sudden concern when Finnegan Scott didn't cry at birth. We waited through three agonizing days of intensive care with our first precious grandson. All of us begged God to heal his little body and let him live. The doctor came in and gave us the news that we dreaded. He wasn't going to survive. It was the first time I'd ever witnessed anguish. Lydia wailed the most mournful cry I'd ever heard. Jerry and I held her in our arms as she slumped to the floor. Nothing we'd ever experienced had prepared us for this. We all sobbed together. That last night, each of us had a one and only chance to hold our sweet baby

Finn. This is what I wrote in my journal: "This precious baby will soon be lifeless and safely in the arms of Jesus: thank You Father for that hope." I gave him a kiss and knew the next time I'd see him alive is in heaven.

Just sixteen months later, the first baby girl of our son, Jared, died. Stephanie was twenty-one weeks along and started to open far too soon. Hannah Grace was born dead. Two of our first three grandchildren were with Jesus. In many ways, this one was much harder for me to process than Finn. I could hardly believe that God allowed another grandchild to die. I struggled with my anger and emotions after this second grandchild passed too. God once again used His Word to bring me comfort and peace. "From the ends of the earth I call to you, I call as my heart grows faint; lead me to the rock that is higher than I. For you have been my refuge, a strong tower against the foe" (Psalm 61:2-3).

I would rely heavily on the Prince of Peace once again when I was diagnosed with a liver tumor. Psalm 29:11 declares, "The Lord gives strength to his people; the Lord blesses His people with peace." Thank God the tumor was benign! The recovery was a grueling eight weeks long. It gave me extended time to pray, rest, and read God's Word. I treasure those weeks because they really taught me to pray and trust His Word. I learned from James 1:2-4, "Consider it pure joy, my brothers and sisters, whenever you face trials of many kinds, because you know that the testing of your faith produces perseverance. Let perseverance finish its work so that you may be mature and complete, not lacking anything."

Many other health problems, disappointments with people, and emotional experiences have happened in the years since I've known Jesus as my Savior and Lord. He has taken me through each day and every trouble by the power of His Holy Spirit. His precious promises in the Word are my spiritual food all day long. Every day gets us closer to seeing Jesus face-to-face in all His glory. We will get to see Him either here, there, or in the air, so be ready because it might be today! Come, Lord Jesus!

Ryan and Melissa

Ryan – While I was growing up, we never really went to church. My dad was a workaholic. As I look back at growing up on the farm, there were a lot of things that taught me about life and death: cattle being born, cattle dying, and eggs hatching. I remember, at times, calves would be in the ditch of water, almost dead. Dad would drag them out, tie ropes on their legs, and swing them around to get the water out of their lungs. We would then take them to the house and put them in the tub to get them warm. They would somehow make it. My dad saved many calves. I don't know where he got the idea on how to do it.

I started going to church before Melissa and I got married. It was a gradual process because it took a while to get to where I am now. I studied the Word and read a lot. I always struggled with the idea of fire and brimstone and the pointing of fingers, but I find that is not how it is at all. Every church is different.

I am always praying throughout my day. I pray for the things I am thankful for, to honor God, and to thank Him for the little things He gives me. In times of stress at work or before a meeting, I pray for help and guidance.

Melissa – I see God in my children. I have had the pleasure of seeing God work in them, and I am so thankful for that. I was blessed to be their Sunday school teacher at church as they were growing up. They each came to me at an early age to have me help them ask the Lord into their hearts. Being there with them and witnessing their salvation brought much joy to me as a mother. Now, as they have grown, I am proud of how they have created a relationship with God. It is wonderful to see God work in their lives and answer their prayers. When they are struggling with a problem, trying to reach a goal, or are nervous about doing something new, I remind them of who can help them. Knowing they have asked God for help and watching the amazement on their faces when He answers and helps them through their challenge is a true blessing.

I used to think things just happen. But now, as I get older and more connected with God, I see how even the little things on a daily basis are all led by God. The people we come in contact with each day make a difference in our lives, and the decisions He leads us to make about our careers, purchasing a home, or sending our kids to school are all about where He wants us to be.

I had plans to not follow my major of study after college and continue in retail management after school. God knew better. He led me elsewhere, which is where I met my current boss of over fifteen years. I have worked with him in three different companies as I follow him in different paths. He has taught me everything I know about accounting.

Ryan and I purchased our first house in the school district I grew up in, which was such a blessing. We were working with a realtor who showed us houses that were not near as nice as what we ended up with in Des Moines. At one point, at an open house, I came across a realtor I fell in love with. We asked him to go through a house with us. He found many things that we didn't notice and suggested we keep looking. We started working with him, and one day, while going through a few houses with him, we came across one in my school district. After going through the house, he looked at us and said, "Guys, I think this is your house." Ryan and I were thinking the same thing. God led us to this house, which is just a few blocks from my parents.

A year or so later, we were blessed with our first son, Evan. My mother was able to be there anytime I needed her, and, more importantly, anytime she needed her "Evan fix," as she called it. My mother and I were very close, and having Evan gave us even more time to be together. She only got to be with us a few years after Evan was born. She passed right after his third birthday. She was so much more than a mother to me. She was my best friend. I regret so much because I didn't say the things I wish I would have said. I just pray that she knew how much I loved her and enjoyed every minute with her.

After getting settled in our new home, the grieving process finally hit me hard. I wasn't getting much sleep as our second son, Gabe, didn't sleep well. I was exhausted, depressed, and wanted to give up. There were days I would drive to work and think about driving the car off the road or into an oncoming semi. Living without my mother, my best friend, to go to and comfort me was more than I could handle. I prayed and prayed, and it just seemed like God was not answering my prayers. I needed sleep, help with Gabe, and help dealing with losing my mother. It seemed like I just didn't have anyone to go to for help. I felt alone, even in my home with Ryan.

By the grace of God, I did make it through that difficult time. He is truly the only reason. I feel, without knowing God, I would have given into Satan and taken my life on one of those days driving to work. Now, many years later, I still grieve, but with God's help it is much more manageable.

Elizabeth

When I was three years old, I made the decision to follow Christ. I grew up in a Christian home, but I don't remember asking my parents for help in asking Jesus to "enter my heart." I told them after I made the decision, but all I remember is that I wanted to follow Jesus. I wanted Him to be my best friend, and I've stuck with that mentality throughout the eighteen years of my walk with Christ. This has driven me to dive deep into His Word and reread the Scriptures. I read it like a letter from my best friend because that's what the Bible is; it's God talking to us.

However, like any friendship, it can get rocky; this was not Christ's fault, but my own. I attended a high school known for partying and teenage pregnancies, so it was easy to look down on those who did it. Instead of acting like a Pharisee, I should have looked at them with a broken and loving heart like Christ looks at me when I sin. I didn't, though. I was a Pharisee, and the sad thing is I didn't realize it until after I was out of high school and into college. I think a lot of the reason I was so prideful is because I had never been tempted like many of the students in my high school were.

I was single throughout most of high school and thought my relationship boundaries were solid. I knew that if I were to ever enter a relationship it would be the godliest relationship. (See how prideful I was?) I thought I could have a godly relationship all on my own. However, that was not the case. During my senior year, I got involved in a relationship, and unfortunately I idolized him and the relationship. It took a priority in my life. The relationship did not draw me closer to God but led to a stagnant relationship with the One I claimed as my best friend. I was leading a double life. I'd go out with my boyfriend on Saturday, overstep my boundaries, and then go sit in church on Sunday like nothing had happened. I felt so broken. I knew it was wrong, but I didn't know how to stop. I was relying on myself for strength and not God.

I went to college with the same boyfriend. Near the end of my first semester, I prayed about it. I told God that I knew this was not a spiritually healthy relationship and that I didn't have the strength to end it. I told Him that if He wanted it over, my boyfriend would have to break up with me. A week later, my boyfriend broke up with me. This answer to prayer hurt, but answered prayer isn't always easy.

Since the relationship ended, God has shown me His grace and forgiveness like I've never seen it before. His cross means so much more to me than it did before. God has grown and matured my faith so much! I love how He has used my brokenness for His glory. God knew exactly what that relationship would teach me, but He also knew it would draw me closer to Him. I know it's cliché, but I am a sinner saved by grace. I am not worth saving, but I am loved so deeply by an almighty God that He thought I was worth saving. He sent His only Son to die a sinner's death in my place, and He rose again victorious. Because of Him, I will one day see my Savior face-to-face and live forever with Him in eternity!

Emily

Growing up, my family attended church, and I went to youth group, but we didn't pray or read the Bible together as a family. When Dave and I got married, I still didn't know Christ. Our first date was July 31. That following year, on July 26, Madison, our daughter, was born. Within one year, we had met, moved in together, gotten engaged, gotten married, had a baby, and bought a house. I was nineteen when we met, and things felt very out of control. I didn't know what I was doing.

My faith changed when death occurred in my life. Our neighbors next door had three little ones. The dad woke up one morning with a knot on the side of his neck. Three weeks later, he died. He had been saying he wasn't feeling well for a while, but he didn't go to the doctor. His wife and I became very close. She's really the one who led me to Christ. I remember calling her up one day and saying, "Tell me more about being saved. What is that?" The main reason we started to go to church was because of my stepson, Matt. His mom started going to church with me as well. She and I took the membership class together, and then Tracy's husband died. We became very close after that. My husband didn't go to church with me, but I didn't feel like I really missed him because Tracy and I went together.

I don't remember who recommended the book *The Power of a Praying Wife*, but I read that. Soon after, my husband came to Christ. He's had a lot of hardships in his life, and sometimes it's hard for him to get over that. I, on the other hand, am drawn closer to God when bad things happen.

We started to go to church as a family when Madison was three. Since then I have changed as a mother and a wife. When I was a young mother, I thought about myself and the things I was missing out on. Now I look at everything as such a blessing. I remember how easily I would lose my temper and yell when the girls were little, but now I can see the changes He has made in me and the patience I have. I don't know how people do it without God. Life is so hard, and I don't think I could get through it without God.

I'm reading a book right now by Beth Moore, and she talks about prayer. She says to begin your prayer with praise, then repentance, acknowledgment, intercession, supplication for yourself, and equipping. It's important to take the focus off you. God already knows what you need. He wants that relationship. In the past, my prayers were always about asking when I needed something. I would also pray for other people, but that's still asking for things. I've learned that, in my prayer time, I need to praise and acknowledge Him and let Him know that He is the writer of my story, and He is in control of my path.

By nature I worry, so it helps when I pray about things. I think 99 percent of the things I worry about turn out just fine. If they don't work out right away, they eventually do. Why am I worrying when He's in control?

Silo Sisters

We were brought up in the Methodist church. Mom and Dad always made sure we went to Sunday school. Our dad was Catholic, and Mom was raised Lutheran, but at the time there wasn't a Lutheran church in West Des Moines, so we went to a Methodist church. Our mother was always such a sweetie and a widow at a very young age. As we got older, we thought, *Why move out when we can give her the money? Why give the rent to a stranger's pocket when we can put it into Mom's pocket?* That was one of the selling points of staying home. None of us girls got married. We have always stayed together, made decisions together, and gone to the same church together.

All three of us have taught Sunday school, but right now we are doing other things in the church. We are part of a church circle that raises money, and then the proceeds go to organizations the church supports or to the needs of the church. There are times when we have not been to church for long periods of time. All three of us feel that you don't have to go to church to be a good Christian. It is how you live your life, treat others, and carry on the work of Christ. That is what we have tried to do.

The way you lead your life and do for others is more than going to church. I've seen people who have never gone to church treat people better than the ones who do go to church. I think sometimes people go to church thinking they are doing the "right" thing. In other words, they are seeking approval from others, not God. There is one heaven and one hell. No matter what religion you are, you are going to travel the same hard road.

A minister we really liked had a lake house next door to us before he became our minister. Mom just loved him. She said, "When I die, I would like to have David do my service." He told us the first Sunday he was there, "I guess I had a calling because I was retired and was not preaching any longer." He told us the church had asked him to come back, but he had not made up his mind. He was driving a truck up in the mountains and had a very close encounter with death. He prayed to the Lord and said, "If I make it through this, I will do Your will." He made it through, and so he came to our church. He called our district either that night or the next morning. We were blessed when he came. He would always shake our hands and smile.

There are all kinds of leaders out there. You just have to pray that they will do good and follow the will of God.

Angie

The theme I want to focus on is "beauty from ashes." When I look back on my life, I can see God's hand bringing about beautiful things out of pain and muck. I picture the image of flowers. To me, gardening has taken on a new meaning. It's a powerful reminder of the way God creates such amazing beauty, majesty, and uniqueness all out of the dirt—the dirtiness of life. Flowers feed on fertilizer and compost, and out of that filth comes such beauty. That's so amazing to me! That's just how God works.

I've been drawn lately to Isaiah 61. Isaiah is talking about how the Spirit of the Lord is upon him to proclaim the good news. This verse is all about God doing these things in and through us. The miracle is that He has given this important job to all of us. It is my life's mission to go to the brokenhearted and to those who are captive and proclaim freedom. It is because of my story, my pain, my "ashes," that He is able to use me to declare His glorious grace.

A lot of my life was characterized by depression, starting in my late teens and early twenties. Depression led to addiction to pain medication as I struggled with migraines, depression, bipolar disorder, and trying to regulate my highs and lows. Addiction led to poor decisions—decisions that should have led to disaster and death. But God never left me; His hand was always on me. As I look back, I am in awe of that. He didn't make those decisions that led me to pain, but He has used them as only He can. Now it's up to me to take that message and hope to other people who are in a similar situation.

Addiction led me to do things I never thought I was capable of, but it also taught me that I am a sinner, saved only by the grace of God, and I am no different from the woman on the street who struggles as well. Treatment opened my eyes to see what could and would have happened if I continued in that life. As I look back on that time, it's so hard to even comprehend that I was that messed-up person. But those memories ground me in my faith and remind me that I am a mess without the Lord. There is nothing good in me apart from Him. All the goodness I can muster out of myself is nothing compared to His righteousness.

It is amazing how He can use my mistakes to create something beautiful that is worth sharing and worth living for. God delivered me from the depths of addiction and the ability to live freely, rather than living like I was bound to a stronghold. Because of my experiences, I have such a heart to give hope to people in the midst of pain and suffering. In all His goodness, He has brought people into my life just so I can share the hope that is in Christ Jesus.

There was a time in my life when I wanted to share my story and tell of God's amazing grace to anyone who would listen. I learned the hard way that not everybody wants to know, so I don't share as often anymore.

I don't want my life and story to be about me. I want it to be all about Jesus and how He rescued me. I want my life to be about His grace and mercy. I want people to see that God is shining through me and living in me. What a gift to be His spokesperson, declaring His beauty!

Bailey

Unwanted, unloved, alone, forgotten… *Who am I without God?*

I remember having a good childhood. I loved hanging out with my family and friends, and I loved being a kid—the long, fun summers without a care in the world. When I was two, my dad fell off a 30-foot roof while working and ruptured two discs in his back, injured his knees and hips, and shattered his foot, leaving him in daily chronic pain. He could never work again. I always saw that incident as a blessing since he could always be home. Life was good.

I was saved when I was in third grade. My Wednesday night Bible teacher helped me. When I was in sixth grade, life started to get rough. I always had a little anger toward God for my grandma getting sick with Alzheimer's and my Opa dying, and then my dad began to miss many important events in my life, like dance recitals and school events. I understood, but it made me angrier with God.

At school I had friends, but they were all in other groups. I never really fit in and felt lonely. After talking to my parents, we decided to transfer to a Christian school for seventh grade. I made some new friends there and liked it, but having a small class took some getting used to. When I started eighth grade, I met a new "friend." She would get jealous of things I did and fought back by trying to do them better. On a Tuesday morning in early September, we got a call from the administrator saying I was going to be in ISS (in-school suspension) for three days for harassing this girl. I immediately started bawling because I knew what I was being blamed for was not true. I felt so betrayed. *Why would this Christian girl want to get me in trouble? What did I ever do to her? Why would God do this? I was going to this school to learn more about Him!* So my dad kept my sister and me home for three days. After a family meeting and tons of praying, we decided to go back to public school. After a call, they welcomed us with open arms and said we were more than welcome to come back.

On Monday, I went back to school trusting that God had a plan, but I still had hidden anger. I burned many bridges before I left, and when I came back it wasn't very good. Many people gave me dirty looks or said, "Why are you back?" It didn't make me feel good. As that year continued, I rebuilt some bridges, and it ended up fine. I spent nearly all of that summer with my friends Jeni and Haley.

My freshman year started off great, and I met many new friends. As the year went on, however, bad things started to happen. A girl I'd been off-again, on-again friends with started the usual. Except this time she involved her entire friend group. Fighting a battle that is five against one is a very tough battle to fight. When people say they get bullied, sometimes you don't believe it because you don't see it. This group of girls did everything to make my life miserable. I was called every name in the book. Most people would never have known it was going on because I hid it from everyone. I would constantly come home crying and not want to do anything but lie in bed and watch TV or sleep. I started to become numb. Then I met this guy. His name was Ryan. It was the first time I was happy, and those girls didn't want that to happen. They continued to get worse, and the name calling turned into more of a problem. The worst possible thing that could be said was said. I was told I shouldn't even be alive because no one wanted me there and I should just kill myself. That hit me hard, and it became harder to keep moving.

Eventually Ryan and I started dating, and the bullying stopped. During my sophomore year, I decided to do cheerleading. When I went to cheer tryouts, all those girls were there. But, surprisingly, they became friends with me. We laughed and forgot the stuff that had happened in the past and had a great cheer season. At this point, I was still dating Ryan, and I was friends with all these girls who hurt me. As a Christian, we learn to forgive. So I did just that.

When school resumed after winter break, things got weird. That week, my fairytale ended. I woke up to who I thought was the love of my life ending things. I took that very hard because I gave Ryan everything. To make matters worse, the day after that whole fiasco started, my friends turned on me again. Those girls started that whole thing all over again. This time, everything got worse. I was constantly called ugly and stupid. They used swear words, and once again I was told that my existence wasn't wanted. Often, when people get bullied at school, it ends there and home is the safe place. I wish I could say the same. As if the name calling at school weren't enough, they started coming to my house and writing those names on my car for everyone to see.

There was no escaping it. Being heartbroken, unwanted, bullied, and depressed, I couldn't eat for days and didn't have much of an appetite for a month. I became very depressed, crying for weeks. I didn't want to go to school because I got so upset and nervous thinking about it. I shut everyone out and did nothing but sit at home and cry. Many people tried to get me to do things with them, but I just couldn't. I caught myself driving one day and breaking down into tears. I started to scream, "WHY GOD! WHY WOULD YOU DO THIS TO ME! YOU KNOW I'M NOT STRONG ENOUGH TO HANDLE THIS!" I felt like the devil had taken over me. I cried even more because I realized that I had let this boy come between me and my relationship with God. I let this group of girls stop me from being who I really was. 1 Peter 5:7 says, "Cast all your anxiety on him because he cares for you." I knew I needed to change, but I was so upset with everything, including God, that I just couldn't.

My mom signed me up for TEC (Teens Encounter Christ). I did not want to go at all. My mom said, "You are going, and if I have to pack your bags and drag you in the car, I will!" So I decided to at least pack my own bags. My TEC experience was not great. I shut everyone out and was so angry and upset that I made myself not have fun. There were times I wanted to enjoy myself, but, being the stubborn person I am, I wanted to prove everyone wrong and not have fun. When I got home from TEC, I sat down and checked my phone. I had all these messages and requests from people I didn't even know knew me. I had so much love and support from these strangers.

God put all these people in my life to show me that I was not alone and that there were people who loved me and wanted me around. I realized it was time for a change. I started getting better. I reunited with old friends and did as much as I could to stay happy. I started to find myself again, and I went back to youth group and rebuilt my relationship with God. Philippians 4:13 says, "I can do all things through him who gives me strength."

Going through all this stuff has made my faith in God grow. It made me realize He works in weird ways. I believe this was His way of getting me to rebuild faith in Him and trust in Him and His plan. I am a lot better now. I'm dealing with life's problems every day, but still growing as a Christian and a person. Proverbs 3:5-6 says, "Trust in the Lord with all your heart and lean not on your own understanding; in all your ways submit to him, and he will make your paths straight." I would not be who I am today without going through what I have. It is amazing how God has worked in me and shown me where my path leads if I just trust and rely on Him.

Becky

Ever since I was little, I have always worried about people, animals, and dying. I think God is showing me a new path in life with Levi, my dog. I think Levi will help me get through life a little easier.

I worry about death, and I always think of it as a bad thing. But I've learned through the Bible and going to church that we will see that person again in heaven. It still scares me because I do not want to die. I want to live my life to its fullest, and I don't want to miss out on any of it. I just don't like the fact that I don't know when it will happen. I wish I knew when it will happen because that would give me the chance to do what I want to do. I just don't want to be in the position of dying and not having lived my life to its fullest.

When I don't get my way, even though I think my way is best, I get upset too. I think Levi will help calm me down when I get worked up. Levi is a true blessing that is coming to live with me soon; he has some growing up to do first because he wasn't born very long ago. I have to wait it out, though, and find other ways to solve my problems before he gets here. My cat doesn't understand the same way a dog would. She doesn't understand why I cry, yell, or lean on her. Levi will be able to paw at me, bark at me, or do things to distract me and calm me down. I can lean on him for support, and I think that will help a lot.

Ryan and LIsa

Ryan – We are the traditional "accepted Christ before we were three years old" couple. We accepted Christ before we even understood what it meant. We are so hesitant with our kids about Jesus and what He did for us because we want to make sure they understand it and come to us with questions. Later in life, Lisa and I both had moments where we thought that maybe we didn't understand and should accept Christ again despite our parents saying we asked Jesus into our hearts. At the time, it felt like it protected us—our parents writing a prayer with us kids. We may not have understood, but at least we were given that information at a young age and then started to figure it out as we got older. Now we are on our own and understand it, and we really want this for ourselves. It's no longer our parents telling us what we need to say.

In the last three years, we've had several transitions occur. I had a job where I was making great money, and we felt really comfortable. At our church, we had been working with the junior high kids, then the high school kids, and finally the college-level students. We loved it. As the students aged and moved up, so did we. We felt like we were in the right place, serving God and following His path. Then we met a few people from other churches around the area who were wanting to combine the young adults together and work on more of a Des Moines young adults group. I received an offer to work for a church in Ames, but I didn't take the job because it was half the pay I was making, and I thought there was no way we could do it. We had two kids at the time and thought about our family as we made the decision.

A couple of months later, I lost my job. I thought, *What are we going to do now?* But it also felt freeing because we had been stuck in that comfortable place and had no worries or concerns when it came to finances. The door was open. That summer I spent a lot of time with the kids while Lisa worked. I prayed a lot. I tried to figure out where God wanted us to go next.

Lisa – I was in a panic because I thought there was no way we were going to pay our bills and that we were going to lose our house. It's funny to see how God uses situations like that for us to see His plan and direction.

Ryan – That's kind of the difference between her and me. I think that whatever happens, God is going to make it work. Whereas Lisa looks at it and thinks, "We're going to lose the house!" Through constant prayer, I knew it was going to be okay. I knew He would provide, and He did.

Lisa – Now he is going to be a teacher. He's happy. He went back to school and got a job. It was God that took that job because Ryan never would have quit it on his own.

Ryan – I spent three years not having a job, going to school, and being a stay-at-home dad. We had our daughter while I was still unemployed. We didn't want to stop progressing our family just because a job was not there.

Lisa – That was the one thing that made Ryan nervous during the whole thing. He thought we should wait. We learned to talk through more things and be more still. It made me realize that sometimes we don't see what God is doing in a bad situation until later. Sometimes we might not have known the answer, but we knew He was in control. He loves us and wants what is best for us.

Ryan – It just shows God's timing because sometimes you think there is going to be a quick decision or sign or something that shows you everything is going to be fine. It took a lot of prayer to figure out if I was supposed to work at a church and pursue that or if there was something different I was supposed to be doing. I think trusting God and believing in His Word during those times provided a feeling of peace because it is all out of our hands. I learned to find trust in God always, even when times get rough.

I think one of the coolest answers to prayer through all of this was when I started to take some classes. Before classes started, I didn't know what I was going to do for a job. I thought, *I could keep working toward a degree, but what degree?* Then one of Lisa's patients happened to say, "There's this two-plus-two program that UNI offers for becoming a teacher, and I think there is a meeting next week at DMACC." Lisa came home and told me this, explaining it was two years of an associate's degree (which I had) plus two years of coursework from the school. It was all online.

I had been thinking a little about being a teacher, but I didn't know how that would work with classes and money and such. So I went to that meeting. It was the final meeting before they were going to start the program. There was a lot of information and things I had to get done by certain deadlines. Everything worked out right on time, and I was able to make it into the program. When I got into the program, I had so much reassurance from people saying, "This is what you should be doing." It seemed like an answer to prayer when I was really not sure what to do. God doesn't always provide us with that light-bulb moment. Sometimes He does, but other times we are left with a choice. It seemed like things were pretty clear, though. So now there are three weeks left before I start teaching for the first time.

Heather

Today I see God around me everywhere: in the clouds, in the sunset and sunrise, in the trees, and in the flowers. In some ways, these seem like the obvious places to see God and to be reminded of His unconditional love for me. It took me some time to be able to look and see God around me. As a single mom raising two girls by myself, I struggled with depression on and off throughout their early years. I sat in literal darkness much of my time at home, and when I was out I looked down at the ground.

Slowly, with the help of my church family, I got better. As I immersed myself in His Word and grew closer to Him, I began to see Him in everyday things. I learned to enjoy each moment and to look around me and see the gifts He has given me. In nature, I see paintings that He creates new each day. In the manmade art around me, I see the talents that He has given others. In music, I hear His promises.

I once read somewhere that to help with an anxiety attack you should look around you and find five things you can see, four things you can touch, three things you can hear, two things you can smell, and one thing you can taste. I take this to another level and thank God for each of the things I identify. Giving Him the praise helps to ground me.

Take a moment to look, listen, smell, touch, or taste, and give Him the glory.

Angel

I have seen God work a lot in my family and provide for us when we could not. One of the first times happened when I was eight. We had a lot of presents that Christmas. We had food, toys, jackets, and everything we needed. I realized when my older brother went to high school that it had been the students and staff that gave those things to us. It was their quest during the Christmas season every year to provide for families in need.

God was working when my parents couldn't afford to give me what was a simple thing to most people: a backpack. I had to use a small gym bag with the strings attached. A teacher asked me why I was using it, and I said, "We just can't afford to get one." Today thirty dollars might not seem like much, but at the time thirty dollars was hard to come by. My teacher brought me over to her desk one day and pulled out a purple backpack. I was so excited. It served me well for a good four years. I took care of that backpack as well as I could. I was not working so I couldn't afford another one.

Even though I saw these little moments of Him, I questioned whether God was real or not. I was able to really pick up on His presence when my twin sisters were born. I was eleven. My teachers at school knew of our situation—that we didn't come from a wealthy or middle-class background. We were between the low income and middle class. When my teachers found out my mom was going to have twins, a huge surprise happened. We received a free van from a community member. This act of kindness really showed me that God was there. It was used, but it did what we needed it to do. Mom was so worried because she didn't know how she was going to transport all the kids. With the two new babies, my parents would have six kids. Before the twins, we only had a car that had three seats in the back, so the four of us had to squish together.

When a teacher who really cared for me found out about the twins, she offered to give us a crib. People didn't stop there. We were able to get clothes and toys, and I saw God through everything. It was so amazing to see God inspire someone else's heart to give to those in need.

Even though these things all happened, I was still uncertain about God. By the time I was sixteen, my life really changed because God gave me the gift of hope. One day my dad told me, "I am not able to pay for your schooling." At first I was angry and sad because I knew I couldn't afford to pay for private schooling. I was only working three hours at Hy-Vee. He really wanted to keep us at our school, but he just couldn't afford it. I was angry with God and asked why He was making us suffer. My dad encouraged me saying, "There will be a way to get you there." Knowing the love my teachers had for my family, I decided I would go to them again. Dad said, "Because you are confident in knowing what you want and what you need, the teachers will see this faith in you and help you." I went to the swim coach to ask if I could sell tamales at swim meets. That was our family business. We sold tamales, not only at the swim meets, but also at the middle school track meets. I was saddened, though, that no one could understand the struggle I went through in order to be at the high school.

I prayed to God a lot to keep guiding me, and then I came up with an idea to provide lunch to the teachers. I told some of the teachers about my plan and that the money was for my tuition. They were all on board. After getting an email with our menu, they would place their orders. On Fridays, I delivered their orders during the lunch hour. My dad kept saying, "I want you to graduate, and I don't want you to quit."

I received my diploma in August. It took a little while after I graduated, but I paid things off. I did it. Better late than never! I went through the ceremony, and I was surprised to get the Business Award of the Year. I have to thank God for influencing me not to give up on other people. People have given us so much, and I didn't want to let them down. Presently, I am trying to go deeper in my faith. I am reading the book *Entering the Castle* with my dad. It's time for bonding together and meditating on God. I know He is real.

CHAPTER 5

Prayer

When an individual invites Jesus into their life, the old has gone and the new is present (2 Corinthians 5:17). You make a decision to follow Christ and have a relationship with Him. In order to maintain that relationship, prayer becomes a key component; it strengthens the bond by quieting the heart.

> *"And Jesus answered them, 'Truly, I say to you, if you have faith and do not doubt, you will not only do what has been done to the fig tree, but even if you say to this mountain, "Be taken up and thrown into the sea,"' it will happen. And whatever you ask in prayer, you will receive, if you have faith."*
> **Matthew 21:21-22**

Audrey

God is so much a part of my life. I was raised in a Christian home and went to Sunday school and church all my life. I learned that just because my parents were Christians didn't mean I would become a Christian. Mom always said, "If you sit in the garage all day, you are not going to become a car." You do not inherit Christianity; you have to make the decision yourself. I made the decision for Christ at Bible camp. Our counselor shared with us the way of salvation. I knew about it, but I had to decide on my own. One night at camp, the decision was made.

As I got older, I knew I didn't want to date anybody who was not a

Christian. How do you know if they are? You know by their actions. In high school, I was very choosy in my dating life. When I dated Virgil, I felt like this was the guy. I was fifteen. I wasn't supposed to date until I was sixteen, but he asked me to go with him to a Sunday school convention, and Mom thought that was okay. We dated for about five years. I was the only girl he had ever dated. When he was in college, he told me he felt that it was better if we dated other people because he had never dated anybody else. It broke my heart.

Two years later I was in the living room with my mom because some guy wanted to sell me pots and pans. Back then, salesmen would come to young girls and sell things for their hope chests. They not only sold pots and pans, but also dishes and linens. That was really popular. I thought, *What in the world? When would I use pots and pans since I'm not steadily dating anyone?* We were in the room when the phone rang. Mom answered. She came back to me and said, "I think it's Virgil." He wanted to talk to me and go on a date. He realized for sure that I was the one.

After he got his Bachelor of Science degree from Iowa State, we got married and moved to Illinois all within a week. It was a real challenge for me because I had never been away from home, and I was close to my parents. That took a lot of prayer. There I was, living with this guy I'd never lived with before, and he had these habits that I was not used to. He would eat an apple in bed every night before he went to sleep. It drove me nuts!

God hears every prayer no matter what it is, and He will answer. We know He will answer with yes, no, or wait. Sometimes we wait, and the answer might come after our death. Virgil and I read the Bible together a lot, but we didn't really discuss the Scriptures or dig deep. When I was a young mother, he went back to college for his master's degree. While I was pregnant with my oldest, Mike, I realized that I was responsible for this child. We had a young mother's Bible study every Tuesday morning; none of us was working outside of the home.

One time we had somebody in that Bible study whose husband was an alcoholic, and we prayed for him. He has not touched alcohol for years. He's a wonderful Christian man. We had so many answers to prayer. It's amazing what He'll answer. I grew so much in that group. I learned how to be a mother and how to teach my children about God. It means so much when you see your children living their faith. One day I saw Michelle sitting at the playground, and all these little girls were sitting around her. I thought, *What in the world is going on here?* When she came home, I asked her why all those little girls were sitting around her. She said, "I was telling them about Jesus."

When the kids were young, we were on our way to the zoo one day in the pouring rain. When we got to East 14th Street, Virgil said, "I don't know if we should keep going." But we did anyway and got to the zoo. The minute he stopped the motor, the rain stopped and the sun came out. Can you believe that? I heard little voices in the back of the station wagon say, "We were praying the whole time, Mom."

I remember specifically another moment of a special prayer. After Michelle graduated from college, she got a job teaching at a school in Jewel, Iowa. We had to find her an apartment, so we went there expecting to get one. We could not find anything. Finally, we checked at a realtor's office, and he said, "Why don't you try Radcliffe, a little farming town a few miles down? I know sometimes they have rentals." So we went to a school to see a janitor who had a small house for rent. His name was Mr. Top. I wondered if he was related to a woman I used to travel around with. I would play the organ, and she led prayer groups with me. A missionary would speak, then we would divide into groups and go into different rooms to share with the women and pray. Several of us did this for years.

When we asked him about the house, he said he had just rented it. I then asked him if he knew my friend whose last name was also Top, and he said, "Yes, that's my sister-in-law." I said, "Can you tell us where she lives so we can visit?" She welcomed us in, and I told her the situation. She gave us cookies and said, "So you can't find anything? Let's pray!" She led us in prayer to the Lord. "You know the situation, Lord. Michelle needs a place to live. Please help her find just the right place." When she said "Amen," we looked up and saw Mr. Top's truck pull in. He said, "Is that girl still here? The house is available. The people just called. They found another place." It was the cutest house. She just loved it. It was a beautiful answer to prayer.

My Husband of Fifty Years

Virgil worked as an engineer at John Deere and had twenty-three patents. They were always trying to create something new and different, and they were working on a beet harvester at one point. It's usually wet when beets are harvested, so they were having a terrible time getting the beets up from the wet ground. They told Virgil he needed to come up with a machine that would do this. He prayed about that every morning before he went to work, and he read his Bible and outlined it. Then he came up with something unusual. It was a big wheel that kept turning, and it would shake the dirt off the beets. God gave him that design in the middle of the night, and he got up and began to draw. He told me he had prayed about this, and this was what God told him to design. They didn't want to pursue it because they didn't know how they were going to transport it.

They tried other machines; one was his boss's and the other was from another engineer. They tried them in California, and they failed miserably. They had no other choice but to try Virgil's. They built the machine here at the Des Moines Works, and it worked. He got a patent on that one and called it "God's Machine." The last one he designed was the big round cotton baler. He designed a machine that would pick the cotton, wrap it in a huge giant round bale, drop it, and go on to make more. It takes the place of four or five men; one man can operate this. He worked on that for years, and they are producing them now. They used another building for him to work in that was away from the engineering building because it was top secret since it was the first in the world.

I knew something was wrong with Virgil even before we got the bad news. He was forgetting things. He was in his late fifties when he was diagnosed, but I think there were signs before. We were staying at a hotel in Australia, and I could tell he couldn't remember. We would take the bus to sights in Sydney, and he would not know where to get off the bus again to return to the hotel. It was shortly after that when he retired because he was overwhelmed by that trip. He was diagnosed with MCI, mild cognitive impairment, and started on medication. I researched MCI and found out that it generally always leads to Alzheimer's. It's a gradual thing, and over time he became more and more dependent on me.

I lost him at the fair once. I had to pray. He went into the restroom but didn't come out. A nice gentleman went in to check and said he was not in there. He also asked if I knew there were two exits, and I didn't. I prayed, and we found him.

Later on, as the disease progressed, something scary happened, and he knew he couldn't drive anymore. I was preparing dinner and needed to mail some letters, so he said he could take the letters. He left, but he didn't come back. I was supposed to go to Bible study that night. I called a friend at Bible study and said, "I'm all around town looking for Virgil because he has not come back from the post office." I called the police. They came, and soon other people knew about it. People from my church came to stand with me and pray. We had circles of prayer in our front yard. About three hours later I saw him drive up. I said, "There he is!" He had gone south instead of north. He was clear out in south Des Moines. In a way, it was a blessing because he knew he could no longer drive. He then started to bike.

As Virgil got worse, I did see glimpses of his old self. Sometimes we would go to Gilbert at night for concerts. I would drive into the garage when we returned home. He would pat me on the back and say, "Thank you." He would always thank me, even after every meal.

When it came to the end, I just couldn't handle it anymore. You would not believe what it all involved. He became very violent towards the end. He didn't want anything over his head, so dressing him was almost impossible. I wanted to care for him as long as I could. Finally, my kids said, "Mom, we are seeing things." Michelle saw him hit me once and told me I couldn't go on like this. I couldn't shower him anymore because he would not let me. When I couldn't keep him clean or get his clothes changed, I knew it was time.

Several of his caretakers asked me how long I'd taken care of him. They couldn't believe it when I told them eleven years. When he first came to the nursing home, they told me he was in the very last stages. I didn't know that. Why did my doctor not share this with me? I learned more from this nursing home in those two months than I had learned before.

We were married for fifty years. I am so glad we had a fifty-year celebration, even though he didn't really know what was going on. He was happy and enjoyed all the people. It was a good day for him, and all the kids were there. He didn't know my name at the end, but he recognized me. It was a lot of hard times and a lot of tough times, but marriage is for better or worse. We never know what we are going to be faced with. Who would have thought that somebody so intelligent and so brilliant would have this happen to him? I had a lot of great years with him, and I thank God for Virgil's love and kindness as a husband and father. I treasure many wonderful memories in my heart.

There were many times I prayed for patience and love. I could not have gone through watching him die that last week of his life without hope in God! He loved the Lord, and God gave me peace and a blessed hope knowing that he is free from the disease. I know that I will see him again when Christ comes to take me home.

Bonnie

It wasn't until I was twenty-one that I felt like I needed Christ. Suddenly I saw I was a sinner, and that is something I never really thought about before. I had always thought I was good enough. When I was twenty-one, I saw my need for Christ and had to decide if I was going to live for Him or live for myself. I was dating a guy, and I had to break up with him because I knew I had to follow a different path.

Before I was a Christian, I drank a lot and had been immoral. When I was twenty-four, I decided to go to Bible school. One night while there, I had a dream in which Jesus had me sit on His lap. He said, "Bonnie, it's okay. Go on another path now." That really impacted me as I've grown in my relationship with Christ. As I read Scripture, I see that Jesus does reveal Himself through dreams and visions. I didn't know that.

I've gone on a lot of mission trips and am still so astonished by how much God loves me and how much He loves other people. He gave up His position in heaven to come to earth because He loves us so much.

One of the ways God showed His kindness was in how we were able to adopt our kids. We prayed and prayed for a child. We went to court and ended up losing the first baby we had heard about. Bob went back to school. I was so disappointed because I knew we would have to wait at least two years before we could consider adopting. I remember the Mother's Day before Elizabeth was born. I felt so excited because we knew about Elizabeth. Within a period of about six months, we received calls by eight different people who knew about babies that were going to be born. God really encouraged us at that time.

Elizabeth found out about a month ago that she was a baby from a rape. Thankfully, she is a little older, twenty-one, so she didn't take it so hard. Her birth mother told her the story. I wondered about telling Elizabeth, but it didn't feel like the appropriate time. She has known about her birth mom for a long time and has a relationship with her. It doesn't seem like it has hurt her or her self-esteem. Her birth mom was single and had two other kids. She was willing to let her be adopted because she wanted Elizabeth to have a dad.

We prayed again about another child. Because I had been a teacher, I knew I didn't want to have only one child; sometimes they tend to be more selfish and self-centered. I remember sitting on the step when Elizabeth was about eighteen months old. I prayed for a little brother or sister for her. When she was twenty-one months old, we got Michael. We were called the day after he was born and asked if we would be interested in adopting him. The doctor who delivered Michael asked our family doctor if he knew of anyone who would be interested in adopting him. Our doctor remembered seeing Bob at a men's Christian retreat the weekend before and said, "Yes, I think I know a couple." Our family doctor called about 8:30 one morning and said, "Bonnie, how are you? By the way, would you be interested in adopting a baby boy?" I said, "Well, I think so. Bob is gone to the farm, but I will have to talk to him."

I told a couple of good friends that I believed it was an answer to prayer. After the two doctors talked, a Catholic nun walked by in the hospital. She was going to start the adoption process through Catholic Charities Services. If we had heard about Michael an hour or two later, we never would have gotten him because they would have started the adoption proceedings with CCS. We really felt like God's timing was there. It was the second marriage for both of Michael's birth parents. His birth mom didn't even know she was pregnant until she was eight or nine months along. We believe God intervened. Otherwise, we are pretty sure the birth dad would have had him aborted because he didn't want to have any more children. I guess the birth mom cried and cried and didn't want to give him up. We later found out that they got separated. Every year I write them a letter and tell them that we love Michael and are thankful they gave him life. We have been very honest with our kids about their adoptions. We knew we wanted to be truthful with them. We saw God work in both the adoptions.

I praise God for His work within me and pray He will use me for His glory!

Judy

My walk with Christ is a journey. Sometimes the road has been beautiful, straight, and well-defined. Other times it's been dark, and the roads have twisted and turned and taken me in directions I didn't want to go. Sometimes the dark roads led to beautiful destinations, and sometimes the beautiful, straight paths led to dark caverns. It's like that on any journey you take. When Christ began to take the journey with me, the outcome didn't matter so much because He is my traveling partner and knows where the journey is going to lead.

Most everybody believes there is a God. I think that's why there is conflict in the world—because God is different to different people. When I was younger, I knew there was a God, but He didn't impact my life except when I was in trouble or begging Him to do this or that for me. I didn't live my life in a godly way. I wasn't raised in a typical Christian home. I don't want to say it wasn't a Christian home, because my parents knew God, but it wasn't one to me.

I also grew up in the '70s when drugs, alcohol, and sex were all becoming prevalent. I am sad to say that I experimented with all of those. But then, in 1979, on July 4, I visited my sister and her husband in Iowa. Their church was doing a revival. I heard the salvation message over and over at this event. That weekend I was at Big Creek Lake on the beach, and I was talking to one of my sister's friends. We were talking about all the things I had heard that weekend, and she laid out the gospel: that Christ died for my sins, He rose again from the dead, and if I believed in Him (asked Him to be my Savior) then I would live with Him for all eternity. That is when God became Christ to me. I am lucky because I felt a "conversion," an overpowering feeling of difference, freedom, and love. Christ made the belief in God personal for me.

But then I went back to Illinois, and my old lifestyle drew me back into making the same choices I was making before. Living your life for Christ is still a choice when you believe in Him. You still have to make daily choices to follow Him.

On my nineteenth birthday, I thought to myself, *If I don't leave here, I'm not going to be any different.* I needed to remove myself from the temptation to sin. So I moved from Illinois to Des Moines, Iowa. I still didn't make the best choices until I met Doug, who was also a Christian. We dated and then got married. My life there was completely different from before because I was in church every week, and I was around more Christians than non-Christians.

But being a follower of Christ doesn't mean your life is easier. I think that is a false hope people get. There are still issues you have to deal with, and there's still pain, hurt, and anger. The difference is that Christ is in the midst of all that, if you allow Him to be. If you read, study, and pray, the difference is assurance: assurance of grace and forgiveness. I think He makes life bearable at times.

I made my quiet room because I needed a place where I felt safe and secure. I needed a place where I can be deliberate about spending time with Him in study and prayer because I think everyday life is difficult for everyone. The difference is that, in Christ, you have the hope and assurance that this life here on earth isn't all that it's meant to be.

God has made me a stronger person. In my thirties, I went through a horrible depression, and the Psalms were lifelines to me (especially Psalms 16, 18, and 100). I would study and read them many times throughout those dark days. I would read, "I am the Lord your God who takes hold of your right hand and says to you, Do not fear; I will help you" (Isaiah 41:13). It's a visual that I take with me every single day. There are times when I've been betrayed, hurt, scared, or angry, but knowing that He has me by the hand is a huge thing.

Prayer is the connection between us and God. For me, it's a constant dialogue. I love to pray. I love to talk to God, either verbally or silently. I think it's something you grow into. I don't think it's something you are born comfortable doing. The more you read the Word (like Psalms or Isaiah), the more you can use those scriptures to pray back to God. For me, prayer was at first difficult, but then, in the low, desperate times of my life, when I felt out of control and in darkness, prayer was the thing that kept me alive and sustained me. When you can't tell anyone else how you really feel, what you are really afraid of, or what you really want, you can tell Him.

Jennifer coming into our home was a God-ordained thing. We heard that she needed a home from a friend of a friend who said, "I heard you might want to adopt. She's in a Christian home, and they want her to go to a Christian home." God answered our prayer for a child, only in a different way, not the way we asked, but in the way He planned. Then after she came, low and behold, I got pregnant and gave birth to Joey, and then I couldn't conceive again. God is funny that way. He had other plans again and brought Jodie into our lives through a girl in our youth group. All three of our children are God-ordained gifts brought to us in different ways. We would never have imagined things happening that way, but God did.

I love to study and tell other people about Christ and how He can be in your everyday life. But that's been a thirty-year process: fifteen working with youth and fifteen working and studying with other women. We are called to share Christ with everyone, but if we are not sharing Christ with each other, building each other up, studying together, and praying together, then we aren't able to go and share with others. That is the difference between knowing who God is and having a relationship with Him. I have a relationship with Christ, and then the Holy Spirit helps me communicate with the Father. If you don't know Christ, then you don't understand that. That's the sad part of where the world is today; we've lost the relationship part. I can't imagine what my life would be like without that. Eternity in heaven is like icing on the cake, but you have to live everyday life until you are in eternity. You just can't do that alone. People are putting their hope in things that are hopeless. So many people have put their hope in their money, other people, the government, or some other being.

After I pray, sometimes I feel peace, but not all the time. I know He heard me, though. What I've learned is not to be discouraged when I don't have an immediate response or the quiet voice answering me back. Not every time is there a washing over me of His presence. There are other times when He is so real. I like it when God speaks to me in neon signs, where He'll tell me, without a doubt, that this is what I need to do. One of those times was when I was redoing this room and was painting and praying over it. I've always worked with kids, and when I started doing the Bible study for women several years ago, it was out of my comfort zone because I was used to working with children. I felt inadequate and didn't think I was knowledgeable enough. But when I was creating my quiet room, I knew that God wanted me to minister to women.

While I was painting the walls and standing on a ladder, I had a vision of what the room was going to be like, and it was exactly this. It was like

God showed me "this is what it's going to be." It was the neatest thing. Women who needed ministering to would come to my room. We've prayed together, studied together, and walked through difficult times in their lives. If you are sitting in the chair across from me, you are looking at a sign that says *Hope*, and the last thing you see when leaving the room is a cross that says *Amazing Grace*.

Does God show you clearly all the time what He has in store for you? Absolutely not. Sometimes the only person who understands you is Him.

Prayer releases my deepest concerns, my fears, my desires, my anxiety, and my joys to Him. I have the assurance that He heard them, and sometimes He chooses to reveal Himself to me and lets me know that He heard and is answering. If I stay connected with Him and am in His Word or doing my Bible study, that is when He speaks to me most clearly. There have been so many times where we have been in Bible study and the pastor's message the next week was about what we had just studied. We had no idea what he was going to talk about, but it was the same Scripture passage and the same concept. If you talk to any of the women, they will all tell you this. That is how God speaks.

If you are not in His Word, you miss out on so much. Those are the times when He has revealed to me that He is so real. You don't know how amazing He is until you are connected to Him personally. That is what the world is missing and what a lot of Christians are missing. A lot of people who sit in churches know God and hear about God, but they don't have a relationship with Him. Until you have a relationship with Him, you are clueless about how truly amazing He is.

Noel

God has always been in my life, right from the beginning. I was greatly blessed to be raised by Christian parents. My parents were raised by Christian parents, and there were generations of followers before them.

My mother and father taught me how to pray. Like most children, I have early memories of prayers before meals and bedtime. We attended church and Sunday school every Sunday, and we talked about God and Jesus and all the biblical stories throughout my childhood.

Even then, *I* had to make the choice to believe, as everyone must do on their own.

I accepted Christ as my Savior when I was five years old. I was in my bedroom, and I told my mom I wanted to ask Jesus to live in my heart. She rushed over to my bed, and she prayed with me, as she did many times and continues to do today.

Even though I have known God since I was little, I have had struggles throughout my life like everyone. I have made mistakes and moved in wrong directions. I feel like He's always whispered to me, but I have to decide to listen, even if I don't always like what I hear.

Now I am thirty-eight, married, and a mother of three young boys. I know I have a very important role to play in my boys' faith, just as my parents did. My husband and I are responsible for bringing God into our home and for sharing our faith with our boys. We are the most present Christian examples they will know. I'd better do my very best.

I don't always know how I'm doing, but I get little signs from my boys. When my three-year-old was asked, "Where do birds come from?" and he answered, "God made them," my heart smiled. When my two older boys ask me lots of questions—about heaven, about the ark, about Jesus' miracles—I am so thankful they are curious and want to know Him. God is the most important gift I can share with my boys.

Lois

I have a photo of the Florida sunset that means a lot to me. It was taken in early October 2009. Our kids gave my late husband, Lynn, and me a trip to Florida for our fortieth wedding anniversary. Lynn was already diagnosed with Stage IV lung cancer. We knew his time was limited but enjoyed the trip so very much.

If it was not for God and the peace He gives me on a daily basis, I would not be able to face each day. When I lost my husband (February 28, 2010), I lost not only my mate but a part of me. Sometimes it is likened to losing an arm or a leg, but God was with me and gave me hope. I waited almost two years after his death before moving closer to our daughters and their families. In one day, God not only provided me with a home in Ankeny, but also a job. If that was not an affirmation of what God wanted me to do, I don't know how else He could have shown me His love and care!

On October 31, 2014, I received my own cancer diagnosis: Stage IV pancreatic cancer. It had spread to the bones. For three days I could not pray, and this is coming from a person who prays about everything. Then, as if a dam had burst, my confusion and concern became less and I could once again find the words to talk with my Lord.

Through surgery, radiation treatments, and chemo treatments, the Lord has been with me holding my hand. Talking with Him through the treatment, MRIs, and CT scans has been a special joy. He performed a miracle in my life because on June 10, 2015, I received the news that the cancer was gone from the pancreas and had not spread to any other place on my bones. The doctors have said that the cancer may return, and if it does I will deal with it as before—keeping my hand in the Lord's hands and talking to Him about everything. If the Lord, who holds my hand, cared and loved me enough to die for me, how can I not trust Him? Psalm 139 assures me that He knew me before the beginning of time and before I was formed in my mother's womb. He also knows exactly how long I will live on this earth. All my days were numbered before any of them came to be.

That is one reason why the Florida sunset picture is special to me; it shows the wonderful creation of God—the beauty of it and the vastness of the ocean. I am so small, yet this same God knows the number of hairs on my head. He knows my thoughts, fears, and joys. His love is all encompassing if we only believe in Him as our Savior. What a God we serve!

Jean

I was born at home on a farm near Oskaloosa, the fourth of ten children. I was raised by loving Christian parents, and we all attended church twice a week. I made a profession of faith when I was a teenager. While I was growing up, my folks were strict, and we never worked on Sunday. We were not to play ball or anything like that, but we would sneak off and go to the river and swim.

On the farm, there were always many accidents and injuries, but God was there to see us through. Once, my mother was helping my dad outdoors using the elevator, raising corn up to the top on a crib, when a shaft fell off and hit her on the head. There was blood everywhere. My youngest sister came home from school, saw the blood, and passed out. Another time, my dad was helping a neighbor when his clothes got caught in the power takeoff. It tore all his clothes off, and the neighbor had to bring him home naked. My sister drank kerosene one time. We never went to the doctor because we lived away from town. We just took care of most accidents at home.

When I was twelve, I had polio. It took all my strength away, but God saw me through it all. Today people can't even tell I ever had polio. I couldn't get up and walk or do much of anything. My folks would carry me upstairs to bed and did this for over a year. Our school was about a mile from our farm. As I got better, my family would saddle the horse for me, and I road back and forth to school. They took me at least twice a week into town to a woman who would do massage treatments for my muscles. At night I would lie on the bed or couch, and members of my family would work on my arms and legs (like I was riding a bicycle) to keep my muscles going. Today I'm fine, but my arthritis is pretty bad. Through all those things, whenever anything happened, God was there. He sees you through it all.

When our children started leaving the house, I got more involved in prayer. People need to pray daily. When we were on the farm, we prayed before and after every meal. My dad read Scripture each night after our meal. He would read a whole chapter, and some of those chapters were so long. It would get late at night, and sometimes he wouldn't come in from the farm until after eight. By the time we were done with supper, some of us kids would have our heads on the table sleeping while he would be reading.

Since my husband, Willy, passed less than a year ago, I've gotten even deeper into prayer. I make sure I do all my devotions every day. I find that God answers prayer. When I look at the past, I can see that prayer is answered. I would pray for things, and maybe they didn't get answered right away, but eventually, in His time, they did. You need prayer because it works. I was always taught to pray for others first and myself last.

God sends me blessings all the time. When I am needing someone, usually someone shows up within a few minutes. A goldfinch at the bird bath drinking, a red bird eating sunflower seeds, and an unexpected flower blooming brightly are all blessings. The orioles show up every spring. They eat the jam I set out and make hanging nests in our yard.

I see God in the beauty of nature and in the beautiful pictures He puts in the sky of clouds and gorgeous sunsets. I see Him in everything. God is so good to me. He blessed us with a Christian family and healthy grandchildren. I could not live without Him.

CHAPTER 6

Selfless

Putting others first is a sign of a follower of Christ. The people in this chapter love others because they know that Jesus first loved them (1 John 4:16).

"'Teacher, which is the greatest commandment in the Law?'

Jesus replied: "'Love the Lord your God with all your heart and with all your soul and with all your mind.' This is the first and greatest commandment. And the second is like it: 'Love your neighbor as yourself.' All the Law and the Prophets hang on these two commandments.'"

Matthew 22:36-40

Doug

Church has been a big part of my life. My dad's family had the biggest influence on me while growing up. Every Sunday our family's tradition was to go to Grandma's house for lunch and sit at a long table. It was very much a family building time where we experienced the joy of being with family. They didn't have a television, so we just talked and played while the adults sat around and visited. Grandma and Grandpa were very godly people and read the Bible all the time. They set the example of what following God was supposed to look like. Dad and his siblings followed suit because that was the way they were raised. While growing up, it was never an option not to go to church. It wasn't even discussed. It was an expectation.

Growing up with older adults in our church was definitely an influence as well. We might not have been best friends, but a lot of people at church would drop what they were doing and help you out if you needed something. They lived and exemplified what the Christian life should be.

God has been with me my whole life. There are times when He has made Himself known to me in subtle ways. When Dad was about to pass, the entire family was there except Jessica, who had left the room. We were all standing around singing hymns, praising, praying, and celebrating when his heart stopped. As soon as Jessica came back, his heart started beating again. It beat for just a few seconds, and then it stopped.

I had an employee last year lose a baby. Judy was due in January, but the baby died in the womb. I was able to have some good discussions with her in my office about why God would do this. God sent little snippets of comfort to her. If she hadn't been watching for them, and if she hadn't been tuned into them, she would have missed them. During the funeral, while we were at the burial site, a single goose flew over and began honking just as the pastor finished. The timing was right. God's presence was shown to the baby's mother in other things along the way. For example, after the baby died, they were doing some yard work in the back of the house. She looked down and found a heart from a necklace lying there all by itself. She now wears that on her neck.

When they went to pick out the headstone after he was buried, she said she wanted something with a heart. The guy said, "We have something that is kind of what you want, but it also has a bird on it." I get goosebumps thinking about it and how all these things tied together.

Judy's grandpa was a railroad man before he died. What do you think happened as soon as the funeral was over? A black train blew its whistle. Was it a coincidence? I don't believe in coincidences. God does everything for a reason. He is always showing you that He is there. You just have to be still and know.

Life is very hard. I told my wife today that I feel like I am a kite blowing in the wind and that the string has been cut. I have days like that where so many things are distracting me and taking me away from God. It is very unsettling.

I am not a very dedicated Bible reader, but I see God everywhere. God is always present in my life, convicting me of the things I am doing wrong and encouraging me with the things I do right. The day He stops doing that is the day I've really got to be concerned.

Harold and Eunice

Eunice – I think of God as a foundation for who I am. I grew up in a Christian home. Because of the foundation my parents had, they knew church was very important. My dad never talked about his faith, but he lived it. I never heard him say an unkind word about anybody. He was dyslexic. He didn't read very well, so he had to memorize Scripture. The preacher would preach, and Dad would memorize the words.

During my high school years, I never once considered college. I knew we could not afford it. My desire was to meet "Mr. Wonderful," graduate, get married, and have a family. I met Harold between my sophomore and junior years, and we became high school sweethearts. We graduated from high school and were married the following October. God certainly blessed me with a loving, faithful, and hardworking Christian husband.

I know we aren't supposed to bargain with God, but I prayed that if we had children, I would live to see them through high school. I felt cheated in some way by not having a mother (she died when I was twelve). We have been blessed with three wonderful daughters whom God allowed me to see graduate from both high school and college. All three are married to wonderful Christian men and have blessed us with grandchildren.

When I turned thirty-nine and when each of the girls turned that age, I dreaded that year, knowing it was the age my mother died. I have loved being a wife, mother, and grandmother and praise God for the years He has given me. God laid on my heart the importance of praying daily for our children and grandchildren.

My favorite Bible verse is from Proverbs 3:5-6. It says, "Trust in the Lord with all your heart and lean not on your own understanding; in all your ways acknowledge him, and he will make your paths straight."

Harold – I was raised in a Christian home and made a profession of faith when I was a teenager, but I really didn't make Him Lord of my life until I was in my thirties. Since then, He has been working in my life. I look at God as three in one: the Father made us, Christ redeemed us, and the Holy Spirit guides us.

I've always enjoyed helping people. In 1993 I had my first missions project. I went with my brother to Honduras, and that opened up my heart to helping others. It grows on you. Since then, I have made one trip to Mexico to help out in the medical clinic. Eunice and I have done a lot of disaster relief as well. It has been a blessing having God work in my heart. He has put many Christian people in my life.

I look forward to serving Him in the future. I don't feel I am a teacher-type, but I can share my faith by example and by helping others.

Jessica

For as long as I can remember, I wanted to be a teacher. I would teach my sister when we were kids. We would hold class. I would be the teacher, and she would be the student. I got my hands on whatever old workbooks I could get from my schoolteachers. She was such a great sister. She would sit and let me fuss over her and correct her and be in front of the classroom. This went on for quite a few years. Then, somewhere along the way, I decided I wanted to be a doctor or a lawyer instead.

Medicine has always interested me so I thought I would go to Northwestern and start working on my biology major. I can remember that day like it was yesterday. I was walking along campus and talking to a friend. She said, "You know you are going to have to work with cadavers, right?" I stopped dead in my tracks, turned around, and went to change my major immediately.

Being a lawyer never really entered the picture again, as I ran out of money and had to come home. I was dating my soon-to-be husband, Matt, at the time, and I missed him, plus things at home were not going very well with my parents. So I believed I was meant to come home. Not long after being home, Matt and I got engaged and then married. We started our family around the time he got sick with cancer, and that changed everything. I went to community college for a little while, but I got so big when I was pregnant that I couldn't carry my books anymore. Everything was getting really expensive anyway, and I knew I needed to work. So I quit going to school and got a job.

Being a teacher got pushed to the furthest recesses of my mind. I started doing daycare work because I have always loved kids. I started babysitting when I was around eleven years old, and so it was just a natural step for me. Our family expanded when we had our second child. Before we had him, I was teaching as an associate. I was in a classroom with a teacher who taught my sister in kindergarten. The teaching idea started to come back to me. I thought, *You know? I can do this. I can really do this.* I had no idea what that was going to look like. I had over a year of college under my belt, and I said, "I just don't know, God. We have next to no money. How is this going to happen?"

A friend of mine from church was a huge inspiration to me because she had little girls at home and a husband who had chronic health concerns like my husband. I related with her. We would talk sometimes, and she would talk about Grandview College—how it was private and so close. It was the first time college was back on my radar with the potential to really happen. Then our financial situation crumbled to the point where we had to get help to pay for food through WIC. I was so embarrassed because I had to get my children weighed and measured because we didn't have enough money to eat. I was working a part-time job, and Matt was not able to work full-time all the time, so we just didn't have enough. I didn't know what we were going to do, and I didn't think I should be thinking about college right then, but I was.

I can't look back and see exactly where the rationale of it even being a good idea came from, but I just remember going through the college application process and getting the acceptance letter. I also realized that because we were in such a poor financial situation, if it was going to happen, God was going to have to do it all. He did. I got several scholarships, so I was able to go. God put people in my path, professors and students, as well as many other people, that I needed along the way. My husband was very supportive of my return to school, and he didn't want me to work. So, for the next three years, I went to school. I started in 2007, when my son was seven months old, and I graduated with honors in 2010. I thought, *This is for all those people who said I couldn't do it, it's not going to happen, you can't afford it, or once you quit, you will never go back.* That was not the attitude I should have had because it should have been about what God was doing through and for me. It was about Him not just showing up in my life, but saying, "I have been here. I know what is in your heart, and I am doing this for you."

Looking back, I realize God was saying, "You are walking across the graduation stage because, not only are you good enough and smart enough, but you are accepted. You get to teach now. You get to do that thing you started doing when you were a kid." I had forgotten about that. So I started teaching. Other than being a mom and a wife, it is the single hardest thing I have ever done. I felt like I went from being on top of a mountain because I graduated and got a job right away, to the bottom of a valley, not knowing what I was doing. I felt like all the preparation I had done in college didn't prepare me for what I walked into.

I started working at a school on the south side of the city where almost all the families were without something; sometimes this meant not having proper clothes or enough to eat, and that was just the way it was. Many of the children were missing members of their family, being raised in single-parent homes or being raised by grandparents or aunts and uncles. That was the first time I started to see that God's plan for me to teach was more than just teaching children how to do things. It was about showing love. On my own, I didn't love them the way He wanted me to.

It's really hard to admit, but I have very serious OCD about germ phobia. My OCD is so strongly connected to personal cleanliness that I have had to wash my hands repeatedly at times. I have hand sanitizer in my room, and I was thinking, *Okay, God. This is part of who I am, but then You have me in this classroom with all these second-grade students who have germs everywhere. Help me understand how to do this.* I remember kind of freaking out and thinking, *I can't do this.* But I also thought, *I am not loving these kids how You want me to. This is not it.* So I started walking around my classroom and praying over every seat and every child. The prayer that I said and still say every year is, "Help me love them like You do. Help me see them like You do. Help me be the person they need me to be."

I connect with students because of His work through me. The words that come out of my mouth are not mine; they are His. My mouth starts moving, and sometimes I don't realize what I've said. If I go back and try to remember what I said, it usually is opposite of what I was thinking. I started to realize that God was giving me the privilege of seeing Him work through me, but not only that, kids began realizing that no matter what was going on in their lives, I cared about them deeply, in a way that cannot be explained apart from God. The love I now have for my students is something fierce. But that love is God's love working through me in a way that I never thought was possible. The parts of me that I don't like, like having to wash my hands constantly, haven't completely gone away, but that OCD has been pushed to the back of my mind. I can give hugs and high-fives, and kids can touch me without me internally freaking out. God is allowing me to literally be His hands and His feet and love these kids as He would.

The kids I have now are fifth graders. Some are homeless or have family members doing drugs, while other students have come from such difficult homes that they are removed during the middle of the school year into foster homes. For some of my students, I am the only concrete person in their lives. I might be the only love they get.

I'm so thankful that God allows me to be that for them. I just pray that whichever kids walk into my classroom, no matter what kind of personality or background or behaviors they have, I understand they are God's, and they have been given to me like my own children for a short time. I have to let Him do the work, and I have to let go of that control that I want so badly. I am learning to forget about having OCD and perfecting things so He can do what it is He wants to do through me. Letting go of that, for me, is probably the hardest thing to do because it is free falling—trusting that God is going to catch me. I know He always will. We have enough experiences in our lives that can cloud our judgment and make us doubt that. Let go. Let Him do His thing and work in us because He wants to. We are the ones who put limits on what He can do because we have small minds that only think we have big ideas. These "big ideas" are just a small part of the huge picture that God has in place for us. We are just one small piece in a much larger masterpiece.

I am learning a lot about love and letting Him love through me. I am the student in this situation. God is teaching me and reminding me: "I've got this plan for you. Are you going to let Me in to achieve all the awesome things I have planned for you, or are you only going to let Me in a little?" I'm hoping He is going to break my heart wide open one day because I know that I have not let Him in all the way. I'm hoping He will break my heart and use me in ways I haven't even dreamed of.

Todd

A story is told in John 3:25-30 about a conversation John the Baptist had with his disciples. Jesus had recently begun His public ministry, and people were starting to listen and go to Him. The migration troubled John's disciples. One day they came to John saying, "Rabbi, that man who was with you on the other side of the Jordan—the one you testified about—look, he is baptizing, and everyone is going to him." I don't know what they expected John to do, but I imagine they weren't expecting what he said in response to their unspoken question. He answered, "He must become greater; I must become less." These two details in this part of

John's life strike me: the first because of the truth of my heart and the second because of the way John's response clarifies for me what needs to happen in my life.

As I read this story, I find it all too easy to relate to John's disciples' consternation. John had been the center of an amazing work of God for a while. People came to him from all over the countryside. He was given great respect, honor, and popularity. These things, which can be an addictive combination, were also passed on to his disciples to some degree. Having tasted it, the disciples wanted more. I know what that desire feels like. In fact, if I am honest, I have to admit that a hunger for honor, respect, and popularity has been one of the driving factors in my life.

But John points me in another direction. His response, "He must become greater; I must become less," lays out a very different goal for life than the acquisition of honor, respect, and popularity. Based on what he says about how his joy in life is connected directly to Christ's glory, he seems to indicate that, although honor, respect, and popularity may be pleasing, they are not joy giving. Joy is ours only as Christ becomes greater in the world around us and as His light outshines all others.

Bob and Chris

Bob – I grew up in the Catholic church. I had a roommate who was Catholic, so we went to church together. It was one of those things that was a constant in college. Eventually I got lazy and didn't want to get up in the morning, so I stopped going regularly. I also got involved in relationships and met Chris, so it just fell off my grid. Faith has always been there, but it's not been consistent.

My faith changed drastically about ten years ago after a good friend died in a hunting accident. His wife went to church, but he didn't. The church gathered around her and supported her during that time. It was something we saw from the outside. She invited us to church. We talked about it, but we didn't know what to do. We would be going from a Catholic church to a Reformed church, and it was something I wanted to explore. I thought it was a better way to go forward and bring our kids up in the faith. So we committed and started going regularly. Eventually we became members.

The real change for me came when Chris wanted to start up a bus ministry. She wanted to pick up kids and bring them to Wednesday night church. I was reluctant at first but later agreed. It got me to step out of my comfort zone and to follow where God was leading me—to minister to the youth. I began teaching Sunday school and a class on Wednesday night—things I never thought I would do or was comfortable doing. It was not something I had any desire to do. At a consistory meeting a few years ago, they asked me where we thought the bus ministry was going. I said, "I don't know, but I'm going to keep driving until someone tells me I can't." It's just what I feel I'm led to do now—minister to kids while driving the bus.

I don't have a relationship with all the kids like others do, but I do interact with them. Often, I see them out and about, and I can't tell you how many times kids will say, "Hey, there's Bob. He drives the bus at church." I feel like I am having a positive impact on their lives. Most of these kids come from broken homes. They don't have a father figure in their lives, or their father figure is not a good role model. That's what I feel I am doing. I am filling that void, that gap. It's not something I feel really comfortable doing, but it's something I feel led to do. It just all gradually happened. My faith was really engaged when we started going to church and became active in the community.

When I committed to church and found God leading me, He also led me to other opportunities. I began coaching golf, which is something I always wanted to do. Doing it at a Christian school and being an example to those kids has been amazing. I've learned about faith from some of them. I see how they get through struggles of their own and how they deal with them. It's neat to see how strong they are in their faith and the energy that comes from their beliefs.

I've done things I never thought I would do, and I'm doing things that I wanted to do. I think that is one of the blessings that comes from service. Being on consistory has also helped me focus on my faith. I felt like I was not worthy to be on consistory, but once I got in there it allowed me to grow in my faith, and it pushed me to grow. Even though I've been in church all my life, I'm a whole different person now than I was in college. Back then, I went to church on Sundays only. Now it's a part of my life several days a week because I am more engaged with my faith and with Christ. I am listening and acting on the things I am being called to do. It is a constantly evolving, ever-changing thing.

Chris – I went to a Baptist church as a kid. We dressed up on Christmas and Easter, but that was it. I think I was six or seven when I memorized my first verse. It was John 3:16. I memorized it to get one of those little Bibles. I can look back now and realize that, for my whole life, I have been a people pleaser. I want to please people and make them happy. A lot of changes have happened in the last year and a half, and I've realized it is not my job to make others feel this way. It's our job to witness to people about God. Our goal is to put smiles on people's faces after we witness to them. God is the only One who can please me and change me. He can do it through other people, but He is the one we need to look to.

My church is like home to me. It's security. I know it's where I am supposed to be. It's been like that since 2002. I've always loved children, and God has maintained that passion in my life through the bus ministry and Gems on Wednesday nights. Volunteering is what I really love to do, but I feel like there's so much more for me to be doing. I want to go out and be able to witness to everyone, to make fishers of men. That is what we are called to do. I love what Olaf said in the movie *Frozen*. He said, "The sky woke up." It didn't have to. God did not have to make it wake up. I woke up this morning. Well, why did I wake up? That is something I have to figure out—something we all need to figure out.

Craig and Jan

Craig – One of the things that amazes me about God and my relationship with Him is that He has always moved first. He is always the one who reaches out to me.

I was raised in the church. Both Jan and I grew up in the Disciples of Christ Church, but in different churches and on different sides of town. We didn't meet until we were in our twenties. I went to Sunday school, youth camps, and all that stuff, but I didn't really feel connected to Him. I felt like there was a missing link. When I graduated from high school, I left the church for a couple of years. In a very short period of time, I drank and did about everything that I promised I would not do. I got to the point where I didn't know myself anymore because I was not the person I used to be. I was scared and started crying out to God. When I cried out to Him, I would give Him just a little tiny room in my life, and He would give me so much more, and that increased over time.

This change in me brought me into contact with some Christians on campus, and they loved me unconditionally. My older brother was involved in a program at Drake called InterVarsity. Between those Christian kids and my inner spiritual connection with God, I felt loved to death— the death of my bad self. I just wanted more of Him. One Saturday night, I was at an InterVarsity retreat. After the bonfire, the leader of the retreat told us to go out into the woods by ourselves and ask God what the next step in our relationship with Him was going to be. When I did, I heard Him clearly say, "Take off those boxing gloves." I had only come so far, and I was still fighting Him. Figuratively, I took the boxing gloves off and gave them to God. I said, "There's not much of me left and what's left is not pretty." He said, "That's okay." It was an incredible experience. I felt a peace come over me. His grace and forgiveness are pretty incredible. The more I get to know myself the more I see how sinful I am and how loving God is. It just gets deeper, richer, and better. That was forty-six years ago, and the experience of peace grows more and more. I have peace with Him. However, loving and accepting myself for who I am and for who I am not has been a challenge. At times, when I thought He would turn away from me, He didn't.

While I was involved in Christian ministry at Drake, I felt called to full-time Christian service. At Drake, my major was news editorial journalism. I wanted to be a reporter for a metropolitan newspaper, but the more I did Christian ministry, the more I felt called to that. I really liked being used to influence people's lives. I went to seminary and then came back to Des Moines for an internship. That is when Jan and I met, in the spring of 1974. For forty-one years, we have been doing ministry as a couple. We have ministered in four churches in four different cities: Grand Rapids, Michigan; Peoria, Illinois; Kalamazoo, Michigan; and in a small town south of Nebraska. After six years, I decided to leave the pastoral ministry and come to Des Moines to transition into being a chaplain. Now I'm at Methodist Hospital and have been there for almost ten years. I've seen some incredible healing experiences, as well as very sad experiences. I have been there to comfort the survivors of shootings, stabbings, child abuse, and teenage suicides. God allows me to feel with the people, but not lose myself in it. There is protection. As a department, we have learned to take care of ourselves and each other. We make time to tell those stories and to unpack those events so they don't overwhelm us.

I baptized an older woman who had been a believer all her life, but, for whatever reason, she had never been baptized. She knew she was dying. After I baptized her, she said, "I can go now." She wanted to give God that sign of devotion.

Jan – I got polio when I was two and stayed in the hospital for three months. Two weeks before I contracted polio, I broke my left arm. When the fever broke, they exercised my other three limbs, but they didn't break the cast and exercise my left arm. When they took the cast off, my arm was withered and the muscles and nerves had atrophied. Most of the damage is below the break. They didn't think I would be able to walk, but that ability came back. My mom knew what I had before the doctor diagnosed me, but by then it was too late. My mom was very devoted to my therapy—twice a day for an hour at a time. Her hope was that the function of my arm would come back. She worked her little heart out. At the end of massaging me, she would always rub my back, so now I have a fetish with my back being rubbed. She did this until I went to college. She kept hoping I would get better and be able to move my hand more. It didn't happen.

My clearest recollection of God speaking to me was over that. I used to pray every night that my arm would get better. I wasn't upset about it, and I was never bullied. People were always very kind. There were three of us with disabilities in my class; I had polio, one kid had only two fingers on his hand, and another little girl had cerebral palsy. We went to school and did our thing. My mom made a splint that would match all my outfits. One night while mom was sewing, I prayed and asked God, "I just want my hand to be normal. I don't want it to be weird." He said, "It is okay. It's how I made you." I thought, *Okay.* I didn't worry about it anymore after that. One of my neighbors in college told me I didn't have enough faith because, if I did, I would be healed. I thought, *I clearly remember God saying it was okay.* I did have corrective surgery during my senior year in college because I wanted my hand to look a little bit better. They were able to straighten it out. Before the surgery, I could not put my fingers on a table because my hand was all curled up. That was all a big part of my life and a change God allowed to happen.

CHAPTER 7

Always Knowing

There is a comfort in knowing that God is always watching. His people turn to Him knowing that He will direct their path.

"Trust in the Lord with all your heart and lean not on your own understanding; in all your ways acknowledge Him and He will direct your paths."

Proverbs 3:5-6

Vonnie

Ever since I can remember I have wanted to be a nurse. When I was a child, I loved to play hospital with my dolls. Each doll had its own ailment that I would dream up. My smallest doll was a preemie in the neonatal intensive care unit. Some dolls were sick, and others had suffered traumatic accidents, while yet another had been severely burned. I used rags ripped into bandages and strings tied to bottles for IVs. My mother had a laundry basket on wheels that I would use for an ambulance. Our basement was a makeshift hospital, and I was the nurse.

As I grew older, I still held on to that childhood dream of becoming a nurse. In ninth grade, we were given career assessment tests to see what jobs we might be best fitted to do. I intentionally answered each question with the hope of being best suited for a job in nursing. My goal at that moment was not necessarily to be honest, but to provide myself with the outcome I so desired. I did not want to be told by the guidance counselor that my personality was not suited for the medical field.

I'm fifty-three now and have been working in the medical field as an RN for thirty-three years.

What's God got to do with that? Well, I believe He planted the seed, He watered it, and He has caused it to come to full fruition. When it's God's plan or will for your life, it is the most rewarding life there is.

I love my job. God has nurtured in me a true love for people, especially my patients. I don't see them as a job to get done. My work is not just a paycheck. It's a God-given talent and mission to love His people, all of them. My reward is seeing them smile, relieving their stress, calming nerves, explaining procedures, answering questions, making someone feel more comfortable, and, yes, being a servant even to the point of washing feet.

Romans 8:28 says, "And we know that in all things God works for the good of those who love him, who have been called according to his purpose."

Angela

God has provided me with everything in my life. I am thankful for all the gifts He has given me. I have a loving, kind, and generous family that supports me in everything I do, especially my mom, who is right there with me through everything. Not only are my family some of the most supportive people in my life, but my friends make each day even more of a blessing.

Throughout all my adventures, I see God in everything I do.

My career, college path, and college involvement would not be as strong as they are without the strength I feel God has given me since I was born. I am blessed to be able to go to Grand View University where my life is falling into place. My journalism career is branching off and rapidly growing. Here I have begun the biggest transition of my life. God has already shaped who I am becoming, and I feel I have grown in just my first year of schooling.

My involvement on campus is something that requires a lot of motivation, confidence, and strength. I feel that God has given me a gift to be this way and a drive to want to do each of these things.

Lastly, I know God was there for a big decision I made. This year I began a relationship. I cannot thank God enough for giving me the confidence to let things fall into place and to let this person bless my life. At first things were scary. It was something new and exciting at the same time. I feel God was with me through the entire thing, guiding me to what He felt would be good for me.

The list goes on about how He has worked in my life. But, most importantly, I am thankful for being given the chance to make a difference in the world. That is something I work toward each day.

Marla

I was blessed to be raised in a Christian home and baptized as an infant. I have never known what it was like to not be involved in church activities with a church family. Growing up, I didn't always think it was so great to be raised with so many rules, but in the era I grew up in, that was the way it was. At that time, dancing, card playing, and movies were really frowned upon. I now realize that my parents were trying to instill a strong foundation in me. When I was seventeen, I made a public profession of my faith and became a church member.

Even though I had always known that Jesus Christ died to save me from my sins, I don't think I completely comprehended Christ's unconditional love for me until I really began growing in my faith. I came to realize that it's only by God's love, grace, and mercy that I totally accepted what true faith is. Jesus is always right beside me, only a prayer away, and I can always rely on Him. No matter what sin I might commit, I know it's been forgiven, and there is nothing I can do to earn the wonderful gift of eternal life.

Never was I more aware of His presence than when my husband (Marv) experienced so many health issues and had so many ups and downs through the years. Through it all, I knew that God was in control no matter the outcome.

When Marv did pass away, I could be thankful and have peace that he was finally finished with his pain and suffering. He is enjoying his eternal reward, which I will also experience someday. Praise God for His unending love.

Kae

There is a contemporary Christian song that says, "He is the air I breathe." I love that because that is what God means to me. I've been single all my life, but God has provided me with all I need. People have asked me if I get scared when I think about getting old, and I tell them, "He took care of me when I was young. Why wouldn't He when I am old?" I was raised by loving Christian parents who helped build my Christian foundation; they were an example of what Christ's love truly is.

I accepted Christ as my Savior at the Bethany Women's Retreat in 1969, and even though it was years ago, I still remember how I felt. The first words I said were, "I am free." Since then it has been a growth process that will not stop until I die and have reached my goal of being with Him in heaven.

One of the most important things to me is the people God brings into my life. At first I never know if they will be helping me or I will be helping them. I do know it's always God's timing, and it is perfect. As I think about some of the stories, it makes me remember that God never let me feel like a single, childless woman.

Years ago, my best friend, Sharon, had three kids. I was their babysitter and helped raise them. I treated them like they were my own. The youngest, David, would cry to go home with me from church and would even cry out my name during the night. Sharon said that if she hadn't given birth to him, she would think he was mine. They are all still very special to me.

Then there were all my kids in the different youth groups; I was a youth leader for several groups. I still have some of them as special friends today. I don't know what I would have done without the help of my friends Doug and Mike. We all have different gifts and talents. God will use us if we allow Him.

There is another reason why I never felt I missed out on being a mom. I had a close friend, Lori, whose husband left her when she was three months pregnant. I'll never forget the night she called crying and asked me to come over. I was her birthing coach and helped her through the birth of her child. The night Chad was born was a life-changing experience. The moment the doctor handed Chad to me I felt God saying, *See, Kae, this is what it's like when a tiny baby invades your heart in one second.* I moved in with Lori and Chad for the first three months so that I could help. What a blessing for me to have Chad in my life and to see him grow into a wonderful Christian husband and daddy. He loves the Lord and has a wonderful wife and little girl.

Being in the right place and at the right time is not by chance but by God's design. My niece, Heidi, was very sick and was going to be taken to the hospice house. I was with her mom, Deb, the night the ambulance came to take her. God had me go with her and be with her as she spent her last night here on earth. None of us knew how bad she was, except her brother, Wyatt, who had been by her side the whole time she was in the hospital. One time when I went to visit her at the hospital, I told her I didn't know why she was going through all of this and having so much pain, but God did and He loved her. She looked at me with those deep brown eyes and said, "I know, Kae. He does."

God has given me so many very special friends and a loving church family who are always there. I could never be able to share all the stories about each person who has touched me or whom I have touched. I can think about each one and, once again, see God's hand in the timing.

Yes, He is the air I breathe.

Connie

It's interesting to see how God has been a part of not just my life, but Steve's as well. I think back to when I was pregnant with Zach. I had just started a job at the hospital, and I told them I didn't know if I was going to come back. I loved the job. After I had Zach, I took my six weeks off, and about the fifth week I thought, *I don't think I can go back to work.* We had just bought a house based on two incomes, and I thought, *How am I going to tell Steve I want to stay home?* I wasn't afraid of him, but I thought, *How are we going to do this?* I went to him and said, "I really think I need to stay home." He said, "Good. I didn't want to tell you what to do, but I want you to stay home too." I was so relieved, but I didn't know how we were going to make it work financially. We made it work.

We used to have Christmas parties for the kids when they were little. We knew that Christian school was not really an option, so public school is where they went. The parties were a way to witness to their friends and their parents in a very low-key, kid-friendly atmosphere. We had them at our house for all the kids who were in our kids' homerooms, kindergarten through fifth grade. Every year it was the exact same. They all got an invitation at school; no one was excluded. Half the kids came in the morning and half in the afternoon. I borrowed the costumes from church to act out the Christmas story, and they would ask questions. Then they decorated sugar cookies, ate finger Jell-O, and played games. I always invited the parents and told them I was going to read the Christmas story. A couple of parents would always stay, but not many. We realized it was pretty special to the kids, especially after we moved from the east side. They commented, "No more parties?" They just wanted to hang out. Some had never heard the Christmas story before. They were able to hear it at least one time, and we were able to give them that. The kids always looked forward to it. We had the parties in our unfinished basement, and they took home the cookies.

Being raised how I was, there was an expectation. There was no "Do we have to go to church?" It was a half-hour drive there and a half-hour drive back. It was a great way to learn memory verses, and we sang in the car a lot. As I look back on it, it was good family time. Once I got to high school and college, my relationship with God became more personal. Knowing God is always there, even though things are always changing around me, is reassuring. I may question things, but I know that He is always there, even if I think I don't deserve it; I am so grateful and thankful for this.

I have been deeply connected in my personal relationship with Him, but other times I think, *When was the last time I picked up that Bible?* To know that I can pick up where I left off is just like getting together with girlfriends; we may not have seen each other in ten years, but when we do see each other, we can pick up where we left off. That's how I feel with God. I don't have to be anybody but myself. I've learned to go to Him when I am having a good day, not just when I am stressed or having a bad day. He is never going to put me on hold.

Knowing that He loves me is huge, and I have peace knowing that I have hope when I die. It's a peace I can't explain; you just have to know it for yourself.

My prayer for my kids is that they live out their relationship for Christ and be witnesses for Him. Billy Graham's daughter said, "God doesn't have grandkids; He just has kids." We all have to make our own decisions. My children have to make their own decisions. It is God who gives us the opportunity to choose.

Edna

I can't imagine my life without God. I was born into a Christian family and went to church and Sunday school from the time I was a baby. Every day my parents read the Bible to us after meals. I prayed "Now I lay me down to sleep" every day until I got old enough to want to say my own prayer. When I was about eight or nine years old, a teacher at school gave us a pamphlet that said we needed to accept Christ for ourselves, and we couldn't depend on our parents' faith. I went home and, by myself, prayed for Christ to come into my life and change me. I went outdoors, and everything seemed more alive; the grass and trees were so green. I can't believe I never told anyone. I'm sure my parents would have wanted to know. I knew it made a big difference in my life, and I started reading the Bible more frequently after that.

When I felt God calling me to Christian service, I went to seminary in New York City. I received a master's degree in Christian Education and then taught classes in the schools in Virginia. Later I served as a Christian education director. Basically, my whole career was serving God through Christian education.

Christian books have also had a tremendous impact on my life. *The Christian's Secret of a Happy Life,* by Hannah Whitall Smith, talks about living a Christian life. I have found the information in this book to be true. I thoroughly enjoy reading the Bible and good Christian literature. It has always been a joy in my life to play Christian hymns on the piano or organ. I just can't imagine my life without Christ because it's all I've ever known. To this day, I wonder how people live and survive without God and without Christ.

In my ninety-one years of life, these are a few things I've learned:

- When you listen to the news, pray a quick breath prayer: Love us, guide us, heal us, protect us, guide our leaders, forgive us, teach us.
- We desperately need God's blessings: in our personal lives, as a church, and as a nation. Look to Him, trust Him, and seek His presence in humble faith.
- Don't judge people too quickly. You haven't walked in their shoes. Things may be far different than they seem.
- Don't gossip. Pray instead.
- Don't be afraid to admit you were wrong. Confess it to the other person and to God.
- Listen to other people. They know more than you think they do.
- Be willing to go the second mile without complaining or being a martyr. Put Jesus first, others second, and yourself last. This is JOY.
- Don't put it off until tomorrow if it should be done today.

Tomorrow never comes. (This is why I have trouble losing weight!)

- Worry doesn't solve anything. Trust God. He knows your needs.
- Don't make a big decision in a hurry. Sleep on it.
- Be humble. God gave you everything you have.
- Praise God for who He is, not just for what He gives you.
- Love in deeds as well as words.
- Be glad when other people succeed, and tell them so.
- Don't let the sun go down on your wrath.
- God knows your needs and limits better than you do.
- Look out for the "little fellow."
- Stop whining and complaining; thank and praise God instead.
- Be generous with your time, your talents, and your resources.
- Keep praying.

Louie and Muriel

Muriel – I was ten years old when I prayed for a brother or sister. Mom hadn't had any children for a long time after my parents first got married. Then I came along. When I started praying for a brother or sister, I got a sister. Around that age, I knew there was a God, and I started believing.

All through my eighty-one years, I've seen all kinds of signs that there is a God. Our parents were Christians, so our faith has been handed down from one generation to the next through parents and grandparents that took us to church. Our six children are all Christians, their children are Christians, and the grandchildren are finding that relationship with Jesus as well. It is a blessing for my husband and me to see all of this and to have good health. It is all from God; man can't provide that.

We've had some setbacks, but we've gotten through them: minor surgeries, a farm crisis in the 1980s, kids getting sick, broken bones. God is in control of everything, and we know this. We get around pretty easily, and we need to remember to thank God for that. We don't walk with canes or anything.

Sometimes I forget about God, and I forget that He is in control. I remember that, in the past, when I was busy or stressed, God would come to my mind. I would pray "Help," my shortest prayer. That's all I had to say, and God knew what I meant.

He reminds me He is there. I think that things going wrong or getting sick is a reminder of good health and that I should be thankful for that.

Michael

Central to my walk with Christ is my witness within the business community. I have dedicated my life to catering to automotive products and services for over forty-four years. My business is rooted in Christian values.

Owning a family business brings big responsibilities to my employees and me. I have seen many changes, and I have had to wear many hats to continue the success of this business that was established by my grandfather in 1939.

I am proud of what we do. I truly believe that my faith in Christ has played an active role in this business. I like to think that I am not the sole proprietor but caretaker, having a shared partnership with my God. He has always been with me, and I trust His direction. The accomplishments within this business are unbelievable, which shows that God's hand is in it. He has helped me with many of the tough decisions. I pray for God's guidance and direction for any decision that needs to be made, and He gladly gives me what I need.

I am the third generation to operate the company. Today I also have a fourth generation prepared to take the reins. My son and daughters are now preparing themselves for this awesome job.

The legacy I want my children to take with them is that God is in control of this business. I can feel confident in leaving the business to the next generation, knowing that my children are also trusting in God to continue this partnership.

Anna

I am so thankful for the Christian family I was raised in. I became a follower of Jesus Christ at a very young age. I remember asking my mom questions about Jesus and heaven one evening before going to bed. She explained the plan of salvation, and at that point I prayed the sinner's prayer. During my freshman year in high school, our church had a Wednesday evening youth group that I participated in. From week to week, we were challenged to read the Bible and work through the Bible study lesson. I wasn't completing the study from week to week in order to learn—my motivation was to make myself look good. When the youth leader asked who had been completing the study, I was almost the only one to raise my hand. I was reading the Bible and doing the workbook just to check it off the list.

During the spring of my sophomore year in high school, my grandfather had open-heart surgery. He spent the next seven weeks in the hospital due to complications from the surgery. We almost lost him a couple different times. People from my grandparents' church became regular visitors to that hospital room. Due to that and a few other circumstances, our family left the church we were going to and started going to the same church my grandparents were attending. For the first several weeks of attending services, I had tears streaming down my cheeks. The Spirit of the Lord was in that place and ministering to a high school girl who really needed it. For the first time in a long time, I was hearing the Word of God and applying what I heard to my daily walk through life. The Holy Spirit was teaching me, correcting me, and leading me in ways I'd not experienced before. After talking with my parents, and out of obedience to Scripture, I was baptized. I knew there was nothing special about the water I was entering, but being baptized was a picture of Christ's death, burial, and resurrection.

My Christian journey through life has had its ups and downs, its joys and sorrows. But walking through each day with a personal relationship with Jesus Christ makes all the difference. It's not a secondhand experience or a free pass into heaven due to my parents' personal relationship with Christ. My relationship with Christ did not come from attending church from week to week since I was a baby, by doing good works, or by being a nice person. No one is good. I am a sinful and selfish person who is helpless without the blood of Jesus. It's all about a personal relationship with Jesus Christ: asking Him into my heart to forgive me of my sins, denying myself, taking up my cross, and following Jesus. There is no one I would rather walk through life's journey with than my heavenly Father. Jesus is the way, the truth, and the life. Apart from Him, I am nothing.

Becky (center) and Olivla (right)

Becky – I was born into a family of "old religion." Like one with "old money," I had every religious privilege imaginable: church, Sunday school, love, etc. This went back for many generations. It was abundant, extravagant, and ever-present. Much like a playboy who took advantage of his family's fortune, I took faith for granted. It didn't become my most precious possession until I explored and called it my own.

To me, God is wonderful, mysterious, confusing, and exciting. I see Him and His works in others, myself, and nature. He's like the wind. You don't see Him, but you see His results. Sometimes it's gentle and cooling.

Sometimes it's wild. It's all that I need if I just remember to ask.

I see Him in others' faces. I am trying to see Him more and show Him more. I want people to look at me and know there is something different—something not of this world, but something eternal. I want them to know it's because of Jesus Christ and what He did for us.

I'm thankful I grew up with "old religion." I'm trying to share it with all those around me and pass it on to my future generations.

Olivia – I have felt extremely blessed throughout my entire life. I could have been born in a poverty-stricken country or placed with an angry family that abuses each other and yells and fights. Sometimes I find it crazy just how much I have; it almost seems a little unfair.

We live in a society that doesn't see how blessed we are. We have such a negative perspective. Everywhere you look you can see it. People don't see how good their lives are. They just see how bad things are. I'm not perfect. I know I complain a lot, but sometimes I have to stop and think about how little my problem really is, especially compared to how big God is.

I think about the Bible verse from 1 Corinthians 10:13 that says, "No temptation has overtaken you except what is common to mankind. And God is faithful; he will not let you be tempted beyond what you can bear. But when you are tempted, he will also provide a way out so that you can endure it."

This verse has helped me through more situations than I can count.

Laura

He means everything to me. I'm completely lost without Him. I grew up in a Christian home. My mom has always been a Christian. She led my grandmother to Christ, which I didn't know about until I was older. She would read books to me, and I went to Sunday school.

I know that many people go through a time where they doubt His existence, but I never have. I can't even imagine that. However, I spent a great deal of my life being away from Him and not involving Him in my life. I didn't hold myself accountable to Him, and those were dark days. That's the difference. When He is not your center, you rely on yourself and others. It is a constant disappointment, a vicious cycle. Those dark days were when I had a very bad marriage. I was in an abusive relationship for twenty years. Finally, I knew I had to leave; otherwise, he was going to kill me. My children lived through it all, which is sad. I didn't leave until the kids were grown. I lived by "It is yours, mine, and ours." That was the reason I stayed for so many years. When we got married, he had a two-year-old son whose mother had walked out on him. Today his son is in prison and serving a life sentence for murder. It was drug related. I spent all those years trying to protect him from all the turmoil. Not one of my four children is in church, but I pray and I pray, just as Mom did for us.

If I can give anything to my children, my grandchildren, and my great-grandchildren, it would be the knowledge of Christ and to know that all the weight is off you when you know Him. When you have a personal relationship with God, there is nothing like it. You are at peace. Things don't bother you, and you don't care. I don't want to say that I don't value life, but if I die tomorrow, that's okay. I'm not going to worry about it. I'm going to be with Him. That's how I feel about my heavenly Father.

Can I say there was one day that I opened my eyes and my life was changed? I can't. He just slowly let me come back because He never gave up on me. He continues to tap, tap, tap away. I don't have that life-changing day, but I've had some really extreme and dynamic experiences in the last few years.

My pastor spoke about God talking to us. I've never had that before until about three months ago. I was getting so overwhelmed and stressed with work. I didn't know how it was all going to get done, and my Crohn's was bothering me. I went one night with just a couple hours of sleep. The next morning, I ended up sleeping in, past the time to be at work. That never happens. The alarm always wakes me up. The whole day went wrong, and I was more stressed than ever. That night I went home and went to bed. I don't think I was asleep for more than an hour when something woke me up. I don't know what it was. It was like a dream, but I could hear God talking to me saying, *Laura, you are exactly where I want you to be, and you are doing exactly what I want you to be doing. Let go of being stressed.* He talked me through it, and I have been fine since then. The stress went away. I had to share it with my pastor, my friends, and my Christian friends. It was just like a dream. I thought, *Am I awake?* He comforted me. I am His, and He is mine.

Anna

I can't remember a time when I didn't know Christ was my Savior. John 3:16 and melodies of "Jesus Loves Me" escaped my mouth not far behind "mom" and "dad." The church has always been my second home. I've been blessed to be raised by parents who were intent on following God with their whole heart, mind, soul, and strength.

I don't recall a specific moment in time where I prayed the prayer of salvation, but for as long as I can remember, I have stood rooted in the truth of the gospel. At one point in my life, I even struggled with the idea that my testimony was boring because I didn't have a radical *eureka* moment. I've come to see, however, that any story of God's radical grace could NEVER be boring, and my salvation has been a continuous radical eureka. My walk with Christ is just that. It's a relationship that speaks of His incredible grace and faithfulness—faithfulness and grace that grows a child humming hymns into an adult shouting praises. It's a life's story overflowing with His incredible, pursuing love no matter the million and a half times I've fallen away. Though my journey of faith is one riddled with continual snares of sin, bumps of doubt, and crevices of apathy, it is altogether a journey mended and upheld with the sacrificial love of my Savior. Ultimately, it's a journey that has led to the greatest and most valuable relationship of my life, a journey I praise the Lord for every day. Also, a journey that has taken me in directions I never imagined.

"What are you going to be when you grow up?" is a question children are asked from kindergarten. Freshman year brought the beginning of the gravity of that choice, and the beginning of an idea that would be a constant whisper in the back of my mind. During the first chapel of the year, a missionary came to speak to us. His story sparked something in me; a passion and excitement for how God was moving in the world exploded in my heart.

Through the rest of high school, that passion sat, but I'd convinced myself that all that missionary stuff would come years later, as the question innocently asked in kindergarten grew into a suffocating, terrifying roar. What are you going to do after these four years are up? Where are you going to go? Where? What? Why? How? When? These questions slowly grow until you dread them your senior year. That is, unless you're me, who thought I had it all figured out. I knew what I was going to do. I'm a planner so I had the next five years of my life completely planned out: my major, my college, my roommate. I decided I knew the plans I had for myself—until God beautifully wrecked those plans.

I'm fully convinced that our Lord has a sense of humor, for it was in Chicago's O'Hare airport, on my way to visit the college I had already set my mind on, that I was told by a friend to check out a mission organization's website. Landing on Youth With A Mission's website sent that fire God had gently sparked freshman year roaring into a consuming flame. My heart was drawn to this organization in a way I'd never felt before. Somehow that wasn't good enough for me at first, though. You see, I already had a plan and that wasn't it. I plugged my ears, stuck out my tongue, and went straight into a stubborn, resounding NO. For the longest time, I had been setting my own plans for my life and demanding that God get on board with them. All year I had been praying, *Spirit, lead me where my trust is without borders*—as long as that's where I want to go. Letting go of something you've been grasping onto with every fiber of your being isn't easy, but it's completely worth it.

As God persistently nudged the idea in my heart and mind, my grip on my plans slipped, and in the end God broke into my heart, and I finally let Him take control. This release brought incredible peace, clarity, and an intense, heart-exploding excitement. And so, after a few months of prayer, I was finally able to answer that question with confidence I hadn't had before, confidence I didn't even realize I was lacking until God grew it in me. I am about to spend six months away from my family, being stretched and grown, and my faith being tested while serving on a mission field. It is not my own plan, and that is the most breathtaking reassurance. My Savior is forever beautifully wrecking my plans, forever showing me again and again His faithfulness. He is forever the rock I stand on, and that makes all the difference in my life.

Scott and Kristl

Scott – I grew up in the church. God was always there and always a part of my life. I grew up in a very small town, so everybody went to church. If it wasn't my church, there was another one across the street. We either went to one or the other. I always thought that was the way everybody grew up. I didn't know any different.

As I got older, I realized it was not true. When I went into the Marine Corps, I realized that God was always with me. There were times when there were close calls and things could have gone wrong but didn't. At the time of those experiences, I didn't think much of it, but as I look back I know He was there keeping me safe. As I caught that glimpse, I started realizing how important and good He was. He was always there guiding me no matter where I went or whatever I did.

After I got out of the service, I finished school and got a job in law enforcement in central Iowa. God was there guiding us every step of the way. When I worked patrol, my adrenaline was often going and things were happening so fast. I was just going. Not until after everything was done did I sit back and think, *Wow, that really could have gone wrong. That was close.*

One of my biggest memories is of when my team and I were doing an entry into a house. There was a guy in the bedroom, and I was the first one at the door trying to open it. He was holding the door, and I was kicking it trying to get in. We finally got in, arrested him, and found a pistol in the bedroom. Later, when the detectives talked with him, he admitted that he was going for the gun, and his plan was to shoot through the door, which would have been right at me. When I heard this information, I realized God was definitely there protecting me.

Sometimes, while on patrol when responding to accidents, people will pull out in front of me or the roads are covered in ice. Even when driving at only 5 or 10 miles per hour, I hope and pray that I don't end up in the ditch.

Sometimes the wind will blow so hard that I don't even know where the ditches are. We have driven with our car doors open so we can see the center line. During these times, you can't stop and say a prayer. You can't think, *I'm going to a domestic with a gun, and now it's time to stop and pray.* I may say something quick as I am going, but I'm thinking about where I am going, where I will park the car, and if I will be safe. I know, in the back of my mind, that God is there protecting me, and I am trusting Him. After the job is complete, I can look back and say my prayer. I put my life in His hands, and I trust Him. I know He will keep me safe.

Kristi – God has been a constant in my life. There was no magical one-time transformation. He has just always been there for me, through the good times and the bad and hard times. My transformation has been gradual and over the whole course of my life. I have found it's important to always stay constant in my relationship with Him and always be thankful, no matter what the circumstances. I can't forget Him even when things are going well.

When I think back over my career, I can see that He has always been guiding and directing my steps. Every time I needed Him, He provided—sometimes in ways I didn't expect. A woman I connected with said, "Hey, there is an opportunity at the library." So I began working there. Then there's the story about how I got my current job. In summary, the kids were at Grandma's house for spring break, and she has two phone lines; one of them is a fax machine that rings. The people trying to get a hold of me about a job opportunity had only my email address, which was not current. They tried to email but couldn't get a hold of me, so they Googled and found Scott's mom because their fax line used to be the teen line; the number had not changed. One day Scott's mom was on the regular phone line when the fax line rang. Katie didn't realize it was a fax line, so she picked it up and said, "Hello." She thought it was somebody we already knew, someone I had worked with. The guy said, "I need your mom's phone number. How can I get a hold of your mom?" She gave him our phone number, which she normally wouldn't have done because we'd talked about stranger danger.

Scott's mom called and said, "I don't want you to be alarmed, but I think Katie gave a guy your phone number." So again, not a normal situation, but this guy tracked me down and said, "Hey, I need a bookkeeper." I liked my job at the library, so it was hard to think of changing. But I thought, *Well, I will just talk to the guy and see.* It turned into another wonderful opportunity.

All those little things that happened are not just coincidences. It was God working out all those details to make changes in my life, changes I wouldn't have made for myself. Sometimes fear and lack of confidence can hold me back from being in the places and situations where He wants me to be, but when I am open to surrendering my will to His, He can use me in a way that brings glory to Him.

Shelley

Every now and then, while growing up, I thought, *What is wrong with me?* People have these testimonies of knowing the exact date when they were saved; I don't have that. I would think, *Am I saved?* When I was a teenager, it bugged me. But as I've gotten older, I've realized I have this blessing of always knowing. I always knew He was there. I was blessed to not have to hit rock bottom to find Him. It was odd because I thought I was deprived. I was fortunate to have been raised to know God and to always have that security. Getting divorced was probably the first time in my life I had an unexpected shakeup. I remember praying, *I don't know why, but there's a rhyme and reason for it. It's all in Your hands, God. Help me through this.*

I've learned that life isn't always rosy, but God is always there. He helped Steve and me handle our divorce in a way that wasn't as negatively impactful on Nick as it could have been. He brought two wonderful people into our lives who were committed to helping us have a friendly divorce so that we could provide the most positive and unified environment possible for Nick. He brought positive Christian friends into Nick's life. God has been there every step of the way in raising Nick.

While growing up, I was very fortunate to have incredible role models who raised me to turn to God for everything and to trust Him. When I was young, I didn't appreciate this. But now I know I have been truly blessed and my testimony is this: while things haven't always been perfect, God is always with me every step of the way, guiding me out of the mud and back onto the path where He is waiting at the end.

Juanita

My grandma was a Nazarene. She wore the bonnet and had the long dress. We would go to whatever church we could walk to. A lot of times it was an Open Bible church. She would sing in church, and then she would continue to sing outside of church. I enjoyed her so much. She died when I was twelve. That was the beginning of my believing in Jesus, and I've never quit. God has been in my heart my whole life. My brother and I moved constantly. But no matter where we lived, we always found a church. He grew up and became a Baptist preacher.

My parents were never religious, even before they died. My brother made sure they were saved before they passed. My sister never went to church, but he made sure Dawn was saved too.

I have never been without God, and I could not have made it without Him, especially with the trials that have happened in my life. I feel like God is close to me every day; I just wish I could draw my family in. All my kids were raised in the church, and they all know Jesus, but so many of them think they don't need to go to church. They miss out on so much. You have to see what you can do for the church and not what the church can do for you. I know so many people who, while growing up, didn't go to church because they were never asked. This is a reminder to me that I need to invite people.

CHAPTER 8

At Peace

T hings happen for a reason, and everyone is on a different journey. These individuals see the Father as faithful, using situations to mold and shape them into who God has called them to be.

"There is a time for everything, and a season for every activity under the heavens: a time to be born and a time to die, a time to plant and a time to uproot, a time to kill and a time to heal, a time to tear down and a time to build, a time to weep and a time to laugh, a time to mourn and a time to dance, a time to scatter stones and a time to gather them, a time to embrace and a time to refrain from embracing, a time to search and a time to give up, a time to keep and a time to throw away, a time to tear and a time to mend, a time to be silent and a time to speak, a time to love and a time to hate, a time for war and a time for peace."
Ecclesiastes 3:1-8

Ivanna, Dimas, and Yolanda

Ivanna – Presently, God plays a much larger role in my life than before. This is because, in my culture, when I was younger, I was pretty much told what to do and believe. Now I have the choice to believe what I want. I try to talk to God as much as I can, but I am guilty of prioritizing other things.

About five years ago, I went to my cousin's church because a preacher from Puerto Rico was coming. I wasn't too excited about going because I felt like I was betraying God and my Catholic church. The preacher called all the teenagers up front, so I went. He started preaching to everyone individually. When he came to me, my eyes were closed. He started talking, and my mind went blank. He blew on my head, and I fell back. It was one of the most beautiful things I had ever felt. I was crying and couldn't stop. I really had no idea why I was crying. I think I was just overwhelmed by the moment and these new feelings I had. Once I was able to stop, I got up and hugged my cousin. He later explained that what I had felt was the presence of the Holy Spirit.

Dimas (Ivanna's dad) – God has always been my guide. I know He is always there, and I feel His presence. I pray to Him and put my life in His hands. Thanks to Him, I have the family I have always prayed for.

Some years ago, I was driving uphill and, halfway up, my car just turned off. I thought I was going to die. I started to pray, and I instantly felt His presence. He guided me through the situation, and I made it home safely.

Yolanda (Ivanna's mother) – God is our Father, and He is always with us. He is the reason why I wake up every day. Even though I have been distant recently, I know He is still watching over me. I felt touched by the Holy Spirit for the first time the day I accepted Christ as my Savior. The feeling is hard to explain, but it's similar to when a mother comforts her small child after he has been hurt.

Julie

God made me who I am. When I was growing up, I could see the difference in kids who had Christ in their lives. I could tell by how they valued things. As a young person, I thought about how I presented myself. I didn't push my beliefs on anyone. Instead, I tried to lead by example.

Being raised in a Christian home has been part of my life. There was never an "aha moment" of being changed. It was just part of my life. It was all I knew. I think, as an adult, you see how it really makes a difference in your life. It's important for your own kids to have faith. God has been a big part in the raising of my kids. I felt like I was kind of the leader of the pack in getting us in a church. We went to the same church consistently, and then an opportunity came up to get involved with a new church branch. Steve started getting involved and began taking the leadership role. He's very quiet. He doesn't speak out, but he is constantly present and wants to make this church grow. We are in the process of planting a church in Ames. He is a major part of that.

This all came about one Sunday. I wasn't home so he took the boys to church. He came home and said, "There was a man who is going to open a church in Ames. He spoke today, and I was really impressed. I think this is where we need to go." It was Steve's decision. We never went to any of the meetings. We just showed up at the church. That has been a life-changing thing for us. If someone told me that we were going to be doing this, I never would have expected it. He's been a good example to our boys, showing them what he really values.

Steve often listens to the radio. One day he came home and said, "There was an atheist speaking on the radio, and he said, 'If you are a Christian, you should stand up for what you believe in. Why are you being quiet? That is not the way you should be if you truly believe in what you do. When you don't speak up, what are you saying?'" I think this had a big impact on Steve, which may have influenced his decision to help out with this church.

As you grow and face difficulties, you realize your faith is what keeps you going. I keep this slip of paper with me at all times. It says, "Life gives us storms, trust in the Lord." The second part is from Proverbs 22:19. I tell my kids when they are upset by unkind and unfair people that those people do not define who or what they are going to be. I encourage them by telling them that they have so much to look forward to in life and that this is just a small part of the big picture. They need to be strong and pray. I need to have faith that things will work out. It doesn't always work out the way I want, but I am not the one in control.

I know, as a mother, I need to step up. That's where faith has taken me with my kids and how I can help them. A friend of mine at school started taking her kids to church because they had gone to a wedding and her daughter said, "What is that T up on the stage?" That moment changed her. My teacher friend said she was an atheist. That was so hard for me to even comprehend. In the meantime, she has started to go to church and is trying to find out if it is something she wants to explore more. She is taking her kids to give them the opportunity.

Alicia

Therefore everyone who hears these words of mine and puts them into practice is like a wise man who built his house on the rock. The rain came down, the streams rose, and the winds blew and beat against that house; yet it did not fall, because it had its foundation on the rock. But everyone who hears these words of mine and does not put them into practice is like a foolish man who built his house on sand. The rain came down, the streams rose, and the winds blew and beat against that house, and it fell with a great crash.

Matthew 7:24-27

For most of my life, I was building my house on the "sandy land." It wasn't until a few years ago that the storms of life were just too much for me to handle on my own and everything came crashing down. That day, by God's grace, He changed my heart. He picked me up out of the mess that I was in and set me firmly on the promises of His Word. I now live on the ROCK that is Jesus Christ. When the storms come, I stand firm in the grace of God. He is the One that carries me through each and every day.

Allegra

God has given me strength to get through things I never would have gotten through by myself, and He has given me joy through times I never would have thought could be joyful at all.

There have been countless struggles I wouldn't have been able to overcome by myself, but I know God is by my side and won't ever leave me. In seventh grade, I had to have surgery on my knee. I was very fearful because the whole idea of getting cut open for surgery really freaked me out. As I went in for surgery that morning, all the thoughts of what could go wrong ran through my head and scared me half to death. When I walked into the room where I was going to be operated on, a sudden calm feeling came over me, and I felt relaxed and knew that everything was going to be okay. Sure enough, the surgery was a success. Looking back at that moment, it's plain to see that God was in control of the procedure, and He was the One who calmed me.

To me, God means hope. I trust in Him because He has an amazing plan for my life. He has never failed anyone, and He won't start now. His love is everlasting.

"For I know the plans I have for you," declares the Lord, "plans to prosper you and not to harm you, plans to give you hope and a future" (Jeremiah 29:11).

Sarah

The Bible is the Word of God. My faith is in the Lord and Savior Jesus Christ. Two inspirational verses that mean a lot to me and help me through hard times are:

Psalm 34:4: "I sought the Lord, and he heard me, and delivered me from all my fears."

God is my refuge. Jesus Christ suffered for our sins, and His death has allowed us eternal salvation. Without the Lord, there is darkness. With the Lord, there is light in the world and in my soul.

Psalm 34:14: "Depart from evil, and do good; seek peace and pursue it."

God is love. He is peaceful and merciful. Jesus taught us to be the same. As we turn away from evil and seek peace and truth in the Lord, we will be saved. Our sins will be forgiven.

Aaron and Alex

Aaron – So many things have had to happen to get me to this point in my life. It is only because of God's grace that I am where I am right now. The blessings I see every day are just amazing. My parents instilled and encouraged faith in me and helped me realize how important family and values are. At times, while growing up, I just went through the motions: *I am going to church and doing all these things, but what does it all really mean?*

Alex and I are both away from our family. Alex has family in Michigan, and mine are in Minnesota. When I go to work for a strong Christian man, the feeling of family is near because he finds the value of family. I'm on the road, and it's pretty difficult to be away. A lot of construction companies work through the weekend, but he wants to bring everybody home so they can be with their families. He brings support financially, but he thinks of our spiritual well-being too. Before he sends us off in the springtime, he always prays over us.

My boss has a prison ministry where he brings prisoners in to work on the road. He gives them the second chance they need to step out of a bad situation and better themselves. He always hires a variety of people, and you run into all sorts. They all have different stories. Some of them grew up in a family full of violence and drugs, and they might be struggling with that themselves.

I have been blessed to work with all types of people. They won't work there forever, and that's fine, but at least it will be a steppingstone. One guy who started out on my crew was in pretty rough shape. He had a prison sentence here in Iowa. Once he got out of prison, he went to church with my boss in Newton. My boss was able to work with him, and then the guy decided he wanted to be a pastor. He was in seminary during the same time he was on the road doing construction, and it was fantastic. He has moved back into the area and has now started a church.

Alex – I was raised in a Christian/Catholic home, yet by high school I was on the wrong path. I was still a Christian and believed, but I didn't live the life God wanted me to live. I was into drugs and drinking. In my later years of high school, I wanted to go to college, and my grandmother said she would help pay for it if I chose a Christian college. My cousins had gone to Door College, so I had visited before. I met a professor during my college visit and enjoyed the passion she had for teaching. That is what I decided to go into because I wanted to learn from her. But when I started my freshman year, I was still living my life the way I had lived back home.

During my sophomore year, I met Aaron. I think God brought Aaron into my life to push me over the edge and encourage me to leave my past behind and learn from my mistakes. He was a very good supporter. He was loving and understanding, and I needed that. I found a really good group of friends and realized that my friends in Michigan were just people I said were friends. There was no personal connection with them. I think God put those college people in my life to help turn it around. If I had not had the push to leave my hometown or those new friends to keep me at college, I would not have changed. I look at those old friends of mine and see that their lives have gone nowhere. They are still doing the same things. I'm glad I'm not a part of that anymore.

After I graduated, I moved back to Michigan and went through several job losses, but eventually I got the job at Des Moines Christian. I love it: the people, the children, and how close it makes me to God. The job came out of nowhere. I lost my previous job on a Friday. That next Wednesday, I started at Des Moines Christian because that's where God wanted me to be.

This time of loss taught me that I need to trust that things will work out. It won't always happen that fast, but it was very eye-opening. I had hope. It's hard to have hope during hard times, but I had to trust that something good was going to come out of it, and God showed me right away.

Lorraine

I grew up on a farm, the oldest of five kids. I always wanted to be a nurse, so when I was old enough I headed to Cedar Rapids for a class. It was only miles from home, so I had it made. It was the end of World War II, and they had a program called the Cadet Core. In this program, the government paid for people to go into nursing. I said, "Well, that sounds like a good deal." My poor folks didn't need to pay for me to go to school, so this seemed like the right thing to do. However, the war ended and the program ended, so I didn't even start the program.

I heard about Broadlawns [School of Nursing] in Des Moines. I had never been to Des Moines in my life. My folks and I came up to check the place out. I remember my dad sitting in the business office. We didn't have a lot of money, and I watched him write out a check for my first year of tuition: $152. I almost cried because I thought, *It's so much money. They are spending all this money on me to come to school in Des Moines.* That's where I spent three years being a student.

I accepted the Lord while in nurses' training during a Billy Graham crusade. My family all went to church, but that was the extent of it. It was a social thing. After I graduated, I stayed in Des Moines, and they asked me to be the operating room supervisor. I had that job for six years. Then John came through nurses' training. He was three years younger, and I taught him as an instructor. I thought he was a pretty nice guy. We got married in June, and I got pregnant in July. After he graduated in September of 1958, he trained to be an anesthetist, and eventually a job opened up at Broadlawns. That was God's plan because he was there for thirty-five years.

Over the years, I have seen different ways God has opened up paths for us. Ending up in Des Moines was a miracle in itself. We are so thankful for our six healthy children.

I feel God talks to me, but He doesn't always respond. I pray all the time. I pray at night a lot now because I don't sleep. I've started praying for people I haven't thought about in years and for those who have influenced me.

I'm eighty-seven, but I don't feel eighty-seven. We have no idea how many days we will be on this earth. I don't fear death, just only how I will die. I've always had this feeling of air being gone and not being able to breathe. That's why I don't like elevators or airplanes. I just don't know the time frame, and I don't like to watch people suffer.

My dad died on a Saturday night. He always ironed all the clothes. He said, "I only have a few left and then I will be caught up." So he ironed. At two in the morning, my phone rang, and he was gone. He had had a massive heart attack at the age of ninety-four. He was an old farmer and wanted something to do when he retired, so he took over the ironing.

Two weeks later, my mom died. She had Alzheimer's, and my dad took care of her. Mom was so mean to him, but she didn't know. After he died, I thought, *God, why didn't You take Mom first? Dad could have had some happy years.* He was never able to travel because he was taking care of her. She was nine years younger. I don't like the month of February very well. Everyone close to me died then.

Joe and Sarah

Joe – In high school I considered myself a believer. But as I look back, I believed, but there was so much work God had to do in my life, and He continues to work. It's the process of sanctification, being conformed to Christ's image.

Many times when Sarah and I have sat with small groups or even the pastor, I have said, "I just don't see God. I don't see Him being active. I know He does things, but I don't think it's like that in my life." My conclusion was that God works all over the world in people's lives, but just not in mine. But now I see my limited understanding was my fault, not God's.

While working with the youth, we've shared with them our life story, and one of the things that became very clear to me was that sharing forces me to reflect backwards. God has indeed been very active in my life. The biggest eye-opener for me was getting married, having kids, and completely seeing the world differently. I have priorities outside of myself. You don't get to be very selfish as a parent.

God has done a lot to open my eyes to seeing my sin and shortcomings, and He has made me aware of just how much grace He really has. I have an increased awareness that God is the center. My mind has shifted in the way I understand this. I used to have a very self-centered view. One of my favorite passages from the Bible is so simple that it might surprise some people. It's not even a full verse. It's the phrase "In the beginning, God." He is the center, the beginning of all things, the first and necessary cause that everything else can't have near the level of meaning, significance, or even being without that point. This really centers the way I think about things, and it changes even the way I parent. We discipline our kids so they learn what they need to learn to become faithful followers of God and have a good life as a result. This is my hope.

Sarah – Presently, I feel God is working in me as I work with the senior high youth at church. Seven years ago, I never would have thought that God would tell me, "You are going to get married to Joe, be highly involved in church, and lead the senior high at your church." I had no desire to work with middle school or high school kids. While I was in school, those years were so hard for me. I didn't like kids that age. We kept getting calls from one of the elders at church. He said, "Several people think you would be really great at this." They tried to get us to do it for a few years before we finally said yes. It was at the last minute when Joe said, "I have to call Mike back and tell him yes or no." I just looked at him and said, "Everything in me wants to say no, but I really feel that, through prayer, God is telling me to do this. It's the right time." I had known for a while that I needed to do it, but I kept pushing Him aside thinking it wasn't what He was really saying. I was being selfish. I wasn't listening to what God was saying to do. So we signed on.

It's hard, but it's just amazing to see God working in those kids' lives. They have done so much for me. Watching them in their walk and seeing how much they change from the first year to the last is really cool. People say, "You have a part in that." No, that is all God. To me, they are like my own kids. I just want to protect them and their well-being, even after they graduate. I was so fortunate to grow up with parents who loved me. Some of those kids have been without a parent, or they don't know their mom or dad. One of the kids was abandoned in a hotel room. They continue to stay strong in their faith, even after all they have had to endure, things that no kid should ever have to live through. I have learned from these kids the type of person I am and the person I want to be. Every time I want to quit, I feel God calling us to stay.

Sarah

An old hymn says it best. "The love of God is greater far than tongue or pen can ever tell. He reaches from the highest heavens into the lowest hell. The guilty one bowed with care He gave His Son to win, His erring child He reconciled and pardoned from His sin. Could we with ink the ocean fill and every man a scribe by trade to tell the love of God above would drain the ocean dry. Nor could the scroll contain the whole thought stretched from sky to sky."

The greatest gift God has given me is the gift of salvation. It is a gift freely given, and I cannot imagine what my life would look like had He not chosen me to be one of His children.

About nine months ago, I was in a very dark place spiritually. I felt like a dry, empty shell, but the Holy Spirit told me to keep on. Even when I didn't know it, the Holy Spirit was moving and active in my life preparing me for what was to come, and, let me tell you, it was worth the wait.

Through reading and studying the Scriptures, time spent in prayer, and the time others spent in prayer on my behalf, God renewed my spirit within me. I now no longer live in fear or darkness. He has opened my eyes to more clearly see His hand at work in my life and others. I feel so alive, and the Holy Spirit has placed a fire in my heart and on my tongue. The freedom I am now experiencing has enabled me to be bold about my faith and to tell others what God is doing in my life and how exciting it is to me.

I cannot wait each day to spend time with Him in fellowship, something I have never experienced before, even though I have been a Christian for as long as I can remember. I feel more alive than I ever have.

God has completely changed my life. I see more and more of my old self dying to Christ every day. I am amazed that I am able to have this happen. For so long, I wanted to hold on to all of it because I thought I could do a much better job of managing my life than God. Oh, what a fool I was. Not having to worry about that anymore is such a blessing.

My life has been transformed by the saving grace of God, and I will not tire of telling others what He has done in my life.

Stacey

We thought we had our paths carved out. Then all of a sudden God showed up. He was calling us to something different. We didn't know exactly how things were going to work out, but they did.

God started working in my professional life. I took a shot at a new position at my current school this year. It was a bit scary for me to be pulled out of the classroom and into an instruction role coach. When the job became available, I remember praying multiple times about whether I should submit my application and letter of interest. *Just be silent*, I told myself. *Just let God talk to me.*

Mike knew I didn't want to be pulled in so many directions as a teacher anymore. He went and searched online and found a job that was being offered in our hometown. He knew how frustrated and upset I was. After looking at the job, he thought I would be well-qualified for it.

At that point in time, he was going to go out fishing for the weekend with his dad, and I was left to decide if I would apply for the job. I decided I was going to apply, and he was okay with that. I submitted all my information. Then, on Friday afternoon of that same week, I was called and offered an interview for the position as master teacher. On Tuesday of that following week, I was called for an interview, and from that Wednesday to Friday, my perspective started to change. The opportunity to come back home? To concentrate on one thing as this coordinator? Then Mike got home and said, "I thought we decided if you got an offer on that position, we would just stay here." I said, "Yeah, that is kind of the way it was when you left. But when you left, it gave me the opportunity to reflect and think and pray about what it is that God wants me to do and where He is calling me to go." Mike said, "I don't think He's calling me to go."

His current situation was very comfortable. He loved his job, the people he worked with, and the financial aspect of it. We were feeling two different things.

We both agreed there was no harm in going through the interview process, so I went through the interview. That very same day they called and offered me the position. I now had two jobs, and one of them was probably about to change. I asked God, "What do You want me to do?" I just felt so conflicted. As silly as it sounds, I went on Pinterest and looked up Bible verses, hoping they would just speak to me.

I told the school in our hometown that I needed more time to think about the job offer. Mike really wanted to stay here. He said that if I wanted to take this job, I was going to have to commute. A few days later, on a Thursday, I decided I was going to turn down the position back home. That morning, before I was about to turn down the commuting job, Mike texted me and said, "Call me as soon as you can." I called him, and he said, "I was pulled into the office and told my job description was going to change." His responsibilities were going to be different. "Accept the job," he said.

My whole body was shaking. I felt like I was convulsing. It must've been enough for him. It was just never clear before. Nothing had made him feel like taking a leap of faith.

We have no explanation for the way things worked out except that God was talking to us. When Mike texted me and I called him, everything just changed. What was best for our family was for me to take this job. It's been so incredible how God has given us twists and turns. One of the things that has come from all of this is that our bond in marriage has been strengthened because of the open communication. I told Mike that maybe that's what this was all about—maybe our marriage needed some work. It put into perspective how much we love each other.

I will not be pulled in so many directions anymore. I have one area of focus: working with business partners in the community to try to find job shadows and internships for kids. I will take kids on events: manufacturing tours promoting local communities and explaining how great it is to work for small businesses. The goal is to bring people back to the communities.

What God has done for us has been incredible. He has helped us make decisions and put us where we need to be. God knows the plan; I just need to surrender control and let Him work in me.

Stephanie

The thing that comes to mind when I think of God is His faithfulness. I think about His faithfulness when He rescued me from my sin and gave me a new life filled with His Spirit. I think about His faithfulness when He provided a husband who loves God and loves me with his whole heart. I think about His faithfulness when He brought me comfort when I lost my first baby girl when I was twenty-one weeks' pregnant. I think about His faithfulness when He gives me strength and wisdom to parent my three beautiful daughters. I think about His faithfulness when He forgives me when I screw up parenting those three beautiful daughters. I think about His faithfulness when He flooded my heart with His peace when I was diagnosed with an autoimmune disease. I think about His faithfulness when He gives me boldness when I proclaim His great name to a neighbor. I think about His faithfulness when He provides a future hope beyond this life. Great is Thy faithfulness, Lord, unto me!

Katie

Through hard, stressful, and doubting times I know that God has always been with me. When my husband and I were struggling to have a child, I knew that God was there, although many times it didn't feel like it. There were many nights when I was frustrated with God, especially when I saw other people having babies. I would struggle to remember that God has a plan for me and that He didn't give me the desire to be a mother for no reason. After three years, we did have a baby, and God's timing couldn't have been more perfect!

Looking back, the timing at the start of those three long years was just not right. There were things during those years that God had me doing that were preparing me for where I am now and for being the best mom I can be. He was preparing me for a job where my kids are with me during each day. I can see them whenever I want, while still having a job to help provide for my family. I know that without God leading me down a path that seemed winding and endless, I would not be where I am today.

Someone told me that the struggles in life are God's way of preparing you for something wonderful and amazing. You learn and grow from the struggles in life, but stick with God and the rewards He will give you (on earth and in heaven) will be well worth it. Where have I seen God in my life? Where HAVEN'T I seen God in my life!

Brenda

God has changed everything in my life: my past, my present, my future. Even before I was conceived, my parents and grandparents were Christians, and God was working in their lives. My identical twin sister and I were born six weeks premature and spent the first three weeks of our lives in the hospital. My mom prayed when we were tiny that God would bless our lives, and He certainly has. Growing up on the farm, I really came to appreciate God's creation and the beauty of the outdoors. I have many memories of playing outdoors with my brother and sisters. We enjoyed all the animals that Dad and Mom had on the farm. We also enjoyed the fireflies and the many beautiful butterflies.

It was hard for me to leave home when I went to college. I was terribly homesick and went home every weekend (except for one) during my freshman year. It was hard to study so much while trying to "fit in" and find new friends. I missed my old classmates, the surroundings where I grew up, and my friends and family. For a while, I was drinking on the weekends and staying out late. My turning point came when my Uncle Arlan, a Vietnam veteran, was hospitalized in the mental health unit at Lutheran Hospital. He was angry, rebellious, and wanted nothing to do with God. After that, I got down on my knees and asked God to forgive me, and I asked Jesus to be my Lord and Savior. I asked Him to come into my heart and to save me from my sins.

Shortly after that, I met my husband. I am thankful that yesterday we celebrated thirty-nine years of marriage. God has richly blessed us with three wonderful children and six healthy, active grandchildren. We have been active in our church and raised our children in and around a loving church family.

Every day I pray that God will help me live for Him. I ask the Lord to continually work in my life and to show those around me His love. My home, my possessions, and everything I have are God's. I don't try to hold onto these earthly things too tightly for I know that they are all temporary.

I look forward to being in heaven someday with my heavenly Father and with Jesus at His right hand. Heaven will be so glorious. I love to read about heaven in the Bible. I will be forever joyful and without any of my earthly cares and concerns. There won't be any pain or sadness. Heaven will be my eternal home. Praise God for His glorious promises! Praise Jesus that He came to earth. God's only Son lived here, suffered, and died for all mankind and me. He rose from the dead and appeared to hundreds of witnesses. He ascended into heaven and is preparing a special place for me and for all who believe and accept Him. May all who read my testimony put their faith and trust in Jesus!

WHAT I LEARNED

God showed me how far I was from Him, and He showed me what a relationship with Him looks like. Before this project I really didn't know Him, I only knew of Him. I knew God was present everywhere and that Jesus died on the cross so we could be reunited with Him in heaven someday, but God showed me that head knowledge is very different from heart knowledge. I had to believe and trust and know that He loves me and has something special to give me. It's called a relationship with Jesus Christ.

When you read Ephesians 2:8-10 and insert "I" into where the "yous" are, notice what happens.

> For it is by grace I have been saved, through faith—and this is not from myself, it is the gift of God—not by works, so that I can boast. For I am God's handiwork, created in Christ Jesus to do good works, which God prepared in advance for me to do.

So He has a plan for me, He has a plan for you. And because I made a commitment to read the Bible, to trust Him, He not only gave me good works to do, He gave me great, unimaginable, unbelievable works to do. He did this to change me, to let the old Lindsay "die" and make her a new person in Christ. I'm living proof that if you read the Bible, study

His Word, pray, and hang out with fellow Christ-followers, you will be changed. My heart has changed, and the joy I have is indescribable.

I look forward every day to spending time with my Lord. Often, when I read the Bible, I want to jump up and down from the excitement His words cause in my heart because they change me.

Praying to my Father is a gift. It's time etched out of my day to quiet myself and speak to the One who truly loves me—and He wants to spend time with me, a sinner who does terrible things! But He forgives. He forgives. We just need to humble ourselves and come to Him and ask for forgiveness.

Before I close, I would like to say that these stories were from God's people. But it's important to know that they came after I made a commitment to follow, trust, and obey Him. He has a plan, and He has things prepared for us, but He wants one thing first: a relationship with Him. Jesus said in Mark 11:23-24:

> Truly I tell you, if anyone says to this mountain, "Go, throw yourself into the sea," and does not doubt in their heart but believes that what they say will happen, it will be done for them. Therefore I tell you, whatever you ask for in prayer, believe that you have received it, and it will be yours.

It happened to me, and it can happen to you; just trust in the Lord.

ABOUT THE AUTHOR

Lindsay Schuling Cooper's purpose in creating this, her first book, is to empower readers with the knowledge that God does work in the lives of His people and loves them greatly despite their sin, imperfections, and faults. Through many trials of her own, she too faced the truth that God loves her and has a purpose for her on this earth.

Lindsay has had a passion for photography since the age of sixteen. She has traveled across the United States capturing the beauty of God's creation through her camera lens. She has taught art and photography for the last twelve years in Des Moines, Iowa, and resides in Ankeny, Iowa, with her husband and three kids, Harper, Calvin, and Norah.

CPSIA information can be obtained
at www.ICGtesting.com
Printed in the USA
JSHW031344020321
12182JS00002B/93